D1248719

Andrew Carnegie

Also by Alvin F. Harlow

BRET HARTE OF THE OLD WEST

JOEL CHANDLER HARRIS:
Plantation Story Teller

THE RINGLINGS

THEODORE ROOSEVELT:
Strenuous American

Andrew Carnegie

by Alvin F. Harlow

JULIAN MESSNER, INC. NEW YORK

Published by Julian Messner, Inc.
8 West 40th Street, New York 18

*Published Simultaneously in Canada
By The Copp Clark Company, Ltd.*

Copyright 1953, by Alvin F. Harlow
Printed in the United States of America

Third Printing, 1959

Library of Congress Catalog Card No. 53-10503

Acknowledgments

My sincere thanks are due to Mr. Carnegie's daughter, Mrs. Roswell Miller, Jr., for permission to use her father's autobiography (published by Houghton, Mifflin Co., Boston, in 1920 and copyrighted by Mrs. Andrew Carnegie) in the preparation of this work.

I also owe much to my conversations with the late Charles M. Schwab.

ALVIN F. HARLOW

Contents

CHAPTER   PAGE

Chapter	Title	Page
I	Prelude in Scotland	1
II	Years of Trial	13
III	The Messenger Boy	25
IV	Up the Ladder	37
V	The Rolling Snowball	54
VI	Bull Run and Dunfermline	67
VII	The Broken Resolution	76
VIII	The Age of Steel	94
IX	A Memorable Year	104
X	Marriage and the Gospel of Wealth	117
XI	Homestead and Skibo	130
XII	Crisis and Solution	141
XIII	Distribution	151
XIV	Late Afternoon	166
	INDEX	179

Andrew Carnegie

1

Prelude in Scotland

ANDREW ALWAYS CLAIMED AND FIRMLY BELIEVED HE REMEM-
bered that incident, though his elders would protest in later
years that he couldn't have been quite two years old at the
time.

"Nevertheless, I remember it," he would maintain stoutly.
"And it's just about the first thing that I do remember."

The incident was nothing exciting—just his parents and
his mother's brother and sister, William Morrison and Mrs.
Andrew Aitken, sitting with their heads together over a
shiny piece of paper mounted on cloth, about two feet long,
attached to round strips of wood at each end, so that it
could be rolled together. Towheaded little Andrew toddled
up to the group and poked his head in inquiringly. His
father and Uncle William smilingly held the thing a little
lower for him to see.

" 'Tis a map, Andra," said his father.

"Map," repeated Andrew.

"A map of America," continued his father gravely. He always talked to the smallest child as to a grownup. "And there"—he pointed to a dot—"is the city of Pittsburgh, where Uncle Andra and Aunt Anna are going to live. Uncle William is going farther, into the province of Ohio."

No doubt that name Pittsburgh, the name of the city where Andrew was in later life to build his fortune, was the word which fixed the incident in his mind—after it had been recalled to him by his parents.

Andrew was still too young to know what it meant for a family in a little Scottish city—from which few persons ever stirred as far as ten or twenty miles in a lifetime—to uproot itself and cross the sea to start a new life in a vast and unknown country where Indians were still troublesome in the outlying areas and whose government was not yet fifty years old.

"I wish you were coming with us," sighed Aunt Anna Aitken.

"Na, na, Anna!" Andrew's father shook his head emphatically. "Not when we've just moved into this braw house, and I've got four looms going." For William Carnegie was a weaver of linen damask tablecloths and napkins—one of many thousands in Scotland who did their weaving at home.

Dunfermline, where Andrew was born, was the damask center of Scotland, and most of its men were weavers. At the peak of its prosperity, there were more than four thousand looms clacking away in cottages in the town and near-by countryside. A weaver would go to his employer or contractor for materials and a pattern; return home and weave the "web," as the piece of cloth was called, then take it to the employer to receive his pay and get another order.

William Carnegie was an established weaver when he married Mary Morrison in 1834. Their eldest son, Andrew —named in honor of a jolly grandfather whom he resembled in temperament—was born on November 25, 1835, in a stone cottage a story and a half high. William's loom occupied one room on the ground floor; the living quarters were in the adjoining room and the attic. But within a year or so, William—a fine, upright man, though a dreamer—expanded his business. They moved to a larger house, and he bought three more looms and hired men to work them. The weaving rooms occupied the whole first floor of the house; the family lived upstairs.

Long afterward, when Andrew became wealthy, a professional genealogist sought the job of preparing a family tree for him, hinting that it would show he was descended from Scottish kings.

"I am sorry to hear that," retorted the unimpressed millionaire. "My wife married me under the impression that I was the son of a weaver."

He might have added, "and the grandson and the great-grandson"; for the family had been weavers for generations, and he was proud of the line of sturdy, honest craftsmen. True, there were noble Carnegies in Scotland! Carnegie is the family name of the Earls of Northesk and Southesk. In later years, when Andrew had his own castle in Scotland, he and the Earl of Northesk became intimate friends and jokingly addressed each other as "Cousin," though they knew of no family tie and Andrew never tried to find one.

As little Andrew's years mounted to four and five, he loved to sit near the loom as his father tossed the shuttle back and forth while his feet worked the treadles, slowly fashioning the beautiful, shimmering damask with its patterns in white of flowers, vines, birds, scenes, and its intricate borders. Andy adored the shy, quiet father who sang, or rather crooned, old Scotch ballads as he worked the loom—"Boatie Rows," "Lochaber No More," or

"Scots who ha'e for Wallace bled,
Scots whom Bruce has often led,
Welcome to your gory bed,
Or to victory." . . .

Andrew could not remember the first time his father

paused, before continuing the song, to say, "That is supposed to be Robert Bruce addressing his troops as they
faced the English army before the Battle of Bannockburn
in 1314." And sometimes he would add, "Robert Bruce—he
became our King Robert the First, ye know, laddie—was
one of the two men—Sir William Wallace was the other—
who liberated Scotland from the English more than five
hundred years agone." He tossed the shuttle from left to
right and back again. "Bruce is buried in the Abbey here
in Dunfermline . . . he and his queen, and many more of
our kings and queens all the way back to Malcolm Canmore and his Queen Margaret—she who founded the Abbey
in 1075."

Dunfermline was indeed a historic little city, for it had
been the political and religious capital of Scotland during
the Middle Ages. Its palace and some other medieval buildings were now in ruins; only one wall was left standing
of the palace where Scottish royalty once lived and where
Charles I of England was born. But the beautiful, square-
towered and pinnacled Gothic Abbey was still standing—
sheltering the tombs of those kings and queens, including
the revered Bruce. And from Dunfermline one might look
southeastward, across the valley of the Firth of Forth, and
see, on a clear day, the steeples and chimneys of Edinburgh looming through the smoke, fifteen miles away, and
its great castle high on the rock.

Andrew's uncle by marriage, George Lauder, was his favorite kinsman and teacher of history and folklore. Uncle Lauder, a shopkeeper whose wife had died some years before, liked to take Andrew and his own motherless son, George, on historical pilgrimages in the city and vicinity; but, before starting, he asked that they learn something about the places they were to see, so they would know what he was talking about. When, for example, he took them to Lochleven, a few miles north of the city, they knew that in the castle, whose ruins lay on the little island in that lake, the unhappy Mary, Queen of Scots had once been imprisoned by Queen Elizabeth of England, whose throne Mary claimed as great-granddaughter of England's King Henry VII.

Many years later, when he was bestowing philanthropies here and there, Andrew built and endowed the Lauder Technical College in Dunfermline in memory of this beloved uncle. George Lauder, Jr., and Andrew also maintained a lifelong mutual devotion. In early childhood neither of them could pronounce the other's name—the best that Andy could do with "George" was "Dod," while George shortened "Carnegie" to "Naig"; and they called each other and signed their letters to each other "Dod" and "Naig" for the rest of their lives.

When they were about six they were taken to Edinburgh to see young Queen Victoria, who was making a visit to her northern realm of Scotland. She was English—a "South-ron" queening it over a land which the two patriotic young Scots thought should have its own monarch—and they looked upon her with coldly critical eyes.

"She's na sae tall as your mither," said Dod.

"And her gown is na sae braw [pretty]," added Naig—glancing at his mother, who had accompanied them.

As he grew older, Andrew's attitude toward England would mellow and he would develop many close friend-ships among eminent and titled Englishmen and their fam-ilies. But in boyhood he was an uncompromising Scottish partisan.

The artisans and shopkeepers of Dunfermline were read-ers and thinkers and did much debating on current topics, especially on politics and religion; for there were all shades of opinion among them, from conservative to radical. Wil-liam Carnegie was one of five men who pooled their little shelves of books and lent the volumes to anyone with a thirst for reading; so Andrew evidently came by his urge to create libraries quite naturally. He himself had the typical Scot's devotion to the poems of Robert Burns—a devotion which was lifelong and unwavering—and, in youth, Sir Walter Scott stood second among his literary heroes.

His father's love of reading at times interfered with his work. He was an ardent admirer of Dickens's novels, which were then being issued in monthly parts—pamphlets of

7

thirty-two pages each—and distributed by a local newsman. When this man dropped in with his "Good morning, Andra. Here is the new number of *The Old Curiosity Shop*," Willie Carnegie seized it eagerly and his loom fell silent. No matter how pressing the need for haste with his weaving, he could not resist the magic spell of Dickens. He would sit devouring the story for five . . . ten . . . fifteen minutes, until at last, tearing himself from it by a mighty effort, he would seize the shuttle and start the loom again, clacking furiously. Meanwhile his wife sat upstairs winding the spools of thread—"yarn," as it was called—for insertion in the shuttle, and sometimes rocking a cradle with her foot; for another son had been born, eight years after Andrew, while in between was a girl baby who had died.

Even in his early boyhood Andrew began to realize that the home-weaving industry was declining; factories with steam-driven looms were taking over. Distress among the weavers became acute—some were driven to working with pick and shovel on a new railroad being built through the county; some went to work in coal mines. Three of Margaret Carnegie's immediate family—one brother, William Morrison, and two sisters, Mrs. Thomas Hogan and Mrs. Andrew Aitken, with their husbands—emigrated to America. Impractical Willie Carnegie, hoping against hope, still clung to the old trade and the old country. But one day he came home downcast and said to one of his weavers, "I shall have to let you go, Tammas; there is so little work." Soon another and another weaver was dismissed, and only William was left. One of the treasured looms, which had cost about twenty pounds, was sold, but brought only a few shillings.

A second and a third loom had to go, to get money for living expenses. The family moved into a cheaper cottage, where Mrs. Carnegie kept a little shop—selling vegetables, fruits, and candies. Meanwhile, at odd moments and in the evenings, the loyal, resolute woman was binding shoes for her brother Thomas Morrison, who was a shoemaker—not a mere repairman but a manufacturer of shoes by hand, with several employees; for as yet no shoes were made by machinery. In the evenings Andrew sat by his mother's side, threading her needles and waxing the thread, snatching time for a bit of reading betweentimes. His days were pretty full ones. His first duty in the morning was to go to the public well, a block or two up the street, for a pail of water; here he had to stand in line with several others— women, boys, and girls—for a turn at the pump. Then he spent a long day in school and, after that, ran some errands, which filled the time until supper.

The first penny he ever received from anyone outside the family was given him by the dour old schoolmaster, Mr. Martin, as a reward for memorizing Burns's poem "Man Was Made to Mourn." Uncle Lauder sometimes gave him a penny, too, for memorizing a poem or a passage from one

of Scott's epics. It was the custom in those days to learn
poems by heart, and Andrew was only one of many whose
lives were enriched by the store of great poetry which they
had at their tongues' ends, ready to be brought forth at will.

Slowly but surely Margaret Carnegie became convinced
that they must try to reach America. The Thomas Hogans
and the Andrew Aitkens were living in Allegheny—a sister
city across the Allegheny River from Pittsburgh (and now
a part of it)—and, though they were not growing wealthy,
they were finding life easier there than in Scotland. Brother
William Morrison was prospering modestly on his farm
in Ohio, not far west of Pittsburgh. Mrs. Carnegie knew
that her husband would be completely lost on a farm, but in
Pittsburgh or Allegheny he could surely find something to
do in his own line. Gradually she persuaded William that
they must take the chance.

But when the remaining loom and the household goods
had been sold at auction, the proceeds were so pitifully
small that the Carnegies found themselves still short of the
necessary cash for the voyage, though one could cross the
Atlantic in the sailing ships of those days for a sum which
seems incredibly small now. The situation seemed desperate
until a lifelong friend of Margaret came to the rescue. She
was Mrs. John Henderson—"Ailie Fargie" she was to Margaret, her childhood pronunciation of her chum's maiden
name, Alison Ferguson. Ailie and her husband had been

putting aside ten shillings a month—about two dollars and a half—toward the purchase of a home. Their hoard now amounted to twenty pounds and Ailie offered it to Margaret, against everybody's advice—including that of Margaret's own brother Thomas, who saw nothing but ruin in store for the Carnegies.

"Oh, but Ailie!" exclaimed Margaret, overwhelmed. "What about your home?"

"That can wait," said Mrs. Henderson. "I couldna do less for the dear friend of my girlhood."

Mrs. Carnegie was in tears. "And John—is he willing?" she asked.

"Aye. The question is, will this be enough?"

"I hope so. By scrimping, we may get through," said Margaret. "And, oh, Ailie, I shall never find words to thank ye! And I promise that the money shall be repaid just as soon as we can scrape it together."

Margaret Carnegie's imminent departure caused much sorrow in Dunfermline; tears were shed over it in more than one home. She had been a wise counselor and friend to all who knew her, and she was always ready with unstinted help in times of trouble. But she was the most resolute of the family in her determination to move to America. Her husband was sad enough, but the one who sorrowed most at parting was Andrew—at parting not only from dear Uncle Lauder and Dod and the other kinsmen, but from the

11

city itself. "What Benares is to the Hindoo," he wrote forty years later, "Mecca to the Mohammedan, Jerusalem to the Christian, all that Dunfermline is to me." He could not feel enthusiastic about America—a country with no heroes to boast of, as he saw it: no Bruce, no Wallace, no Burns. Every last event in Dunfermline was a heartbreak—the last night, the last breakfast, the last mellow ringing of the Abbey bell.

He never forgot the date—May 17, 1848—when they turned their backs upon his childhood home. He was in his thirteenth year; his handsome little brother, Thomas Morrison Carnegie, in his fifth year. On their way to the port in the Firth of Forth, Andrew with wet eyes stood looking back through the carriage window as the familiar landmarks of Dunfermline were gradually hidden from view by an intervening hill, the old Abbey tower last of all. Uncle Lauder, Dod, and Uncle Thomas accompanied them to the waterside. On the wharf Andrew suddenly rushed back to Uncle Lauder and threw his arms around him, crying, "Oh, I canna leave ye! I canna leave ye!" Someone gently drew him away and led him on board the vessel. And so began the transplantation to the New World.

2

Years of Trial

ALLEGHENY, IN 1848, WAS ONE OF THE MOST UNATTRACTIVE
of cities—frowzy, muddy, ramshackle, with littered streets,
tormented by floods almost every spring and an occasional
epidemic of cholera—but it was not disorderly. Andrew
boasted in a letter to Cousin Dod that, although there were
twenty-two thousand inhabitants, its police force consisted
of only four members. A considerable percentage of its
men worked in Pittsburgh, trudging across the Allegheny
River bridge each morning and evening.

The Carnegies were heartily welcomed by their kin, Mr.
and Mrs. Thomas Hogan and Aunt Anna Aitken, all of
whom had taken up their abode on Rebecca Street. None
of them was prosperous, but they considered themselves
well off because they felt secure. Uncle Tom Hogan was

clerk in a crockery store and was making payments on a comfortable little two-story home. Aunt Aitken, whose husband had died several years ago, was now proprietor of a small grocery store. Uncle Tom's brother Andrew Hogan had been living and weaving in a small building on the rear of Aunt Aitken's lot, but was now going to move away. Aunt Aitken offered it to the Carnegies.

"What will be the rent, Anna?" asked William.

"Nothing until you are on a better footing," replied the kindly aunt—and, though Willie protested, there was nothing else he could do.

So now he began his hand-weaving again, just as he had done in Scotland, but with an even greater handicap; for, in America, machine weaving was replacing handwork even more rapidly than abroad. William wove cheaper tablecloths than those he had made in Dunfermline—checkered ones of cotton—and tried peddling them from door to door. Meanwhile his wife went back to her old task of binding shoes—working for a Mr. Phipps, who had a small shoemaking shop near by. Mr. Phipps—with the aid of two or three helpers in the shop and some, like Margaret Carnegie, at home—not only fashioned shoes to order but also made other pairs which at times he would peddle, even tramping into the countryside around Allegheny and Pittsburgh.

By toiling away at her shoe-binding—sometimes until midnight—whenever she was not busy with her housework,

Mrs. Carnegie managed to earn about four dollars a week. It was now little Tom's turn to be the helper. When not in school, often into the evening, he would sit on a low stool by his mother's side, threading needles and waxing the thread, while she recited to him from her prodigious memory some of the old ballads of Scottish minstrelsy or parts of the long poems of Walter Scott. Her reputation as an entertainer spread among the children of the neighborhood; and sometimes there was a group of them around her, listening eagerly while she told them stories from Scottish history or recited stirring portions of those epics of Sir Walter . . .

> "Nine-and-twenty knights of fame
>   Hung their shields in Branksome Hall;
> Nine-and-twenty squires of name
>   Brought them their steeds to bower from stall.
>   Nine-and-twenty yeomen tall
>   Waited, duteous, on them all;
>   They were all knights of mettle true,
>   Kinsmen to the bold Buccleuch."

When the Carnegies first settled in Allegheny, Andrew, undersized, square-jawed, with eyes set wide apart and hair so flaxen that it was almost white, had such a broad Scotch accent that the youngsters of the neighborhood—

known as "Bottom Hooshiers" (from the Allegheny River bottom)—laughed at him and called him "Scotchie"—to which Andy would stoutly retort, "Aye, I'm Scotchie and prood of it." The humorous point of it all was that most of the jeering boys were themselves pure Scotch—the sons of Scottish immigrants—and some of them, like Andy, had been born in the old country. But Andy rapidly lost his Scotch brogue, and within a few months was himself one of the Bottom Hooshiers. Another notable thing is that so many of those boys became prosperous and prominent citizens, and that Andy was able to give some of them a helping hand in getting their start upward.

William Carnegie came home one day from one of his almost fruitless peddling rounds, dropped his bundle of unsold cloths in a corner, and sighed, "It's no good, wife. I canna earn my salt this way. I'll have to take a job in Blackstock's cotton mill." He had already ascertained that he could get work there. He did so, and a few days later said, "There's work for you at the mill, too, Andra."

Andy had been looking for work, but was told everywhere that he was too small. Now he was excited. "What kind of work, Father?" he asked.

"Winding bobbins."

"And am I to be paid for it?"

"Ye will receive one dollar and twenty cents a week."

It seems unbelievably small pay, but Andy was thrilled

by the thought that he would be helping to support the family. Thereafter he and his father rose at dawn—in winter, before dawn—ate a hurried breakfast and trudged away to the factory, to work steadily until six in the evening. The boy endured it better than his father. Willie Carnegie, a dreamy individualist, was wholly unfitted to work for wages, to follow a prescribed routine under the orders of others; and his soul revolted at seeing weaving done by machinery. He quit the factory after a few months and returned to the back-yard loom, thumping out tablecloths and now and then selling one—after miles of walking from house to house.

As the family widened its acquaintance with others from the old country, Andrew met John Hay, another Scot, who owned a small bobbin factory and offered him a place at much higher pay—two dollars a week! It was the most unpleasant work he had yet had to do—in a dark, grimy cellar all day, keeping an eye on a small engine and firing its boiler. He tried to sustain his spirit by thinking how well Sir William Wallace would have stood such a test. No matter how unpleasant the job, he must not let his parents know how he hated it.

Mr. Hay, who had his desk in a corner of his factory and who was his own entire office staff, called the boy to him one day and said, "Andra, are ye good at figures?"

"Why, I think so, sir," was the reply.

"And do ye write a gude hand?"

"Pretty good, sir."

"Let's see ye write. Sit down here." He thrust a pen at Andy and pushed a sheet of paper before him. "Ah, that's no' bad, no' bad!"—as he looked over the writing. "Would ye like to make out me bills?"

"Oh, yes, I would, sir!" exclaimed Andy, with an enthusiasm which revealed how eager he was to get out of that dark cellar.

He little dreamed that something just as bad or worse was in store for him. He was soon doing Mr. Hay's single-entry bookkeeping, but that did not take more than half his time; for the rest of the day he was assigned to the task of giving bobbins a finishing bath in a vat of oil—oil which had such a nauseous odor that he could hardly endure it. Not all his mental concentration on Wallace and Bruce could reconcile him to this, but he gritted his teeth and never let his parents know how he suffered.

In the evenings he sometimes spent an hour at the Phipps shoeshop with John Phipps and other boys, most of them Scotch. One evening, while he was telling about his bookkeeping, Tom Miller said, "Single-entry bookkeeping may do for a small business like Hay's, but all the big companies keep their books in double entry."

This was news to Andy, and he wanted to know more about the better system; but Tom's knowledge of it was scant. A few evenings later, however, Tom reported that he had heard of a man who taught bookkeeping in the evenings for a reasonable fee. After some days of pondering, Andy, Tom, John Phipps, and Willie Cowley decided they could squeeze out from their small incomes the pittances required for the lessons; and thereafter they spent many evenings in learning the mysteries of double entry.

Because of the unpleasant work he had to do, Andrew's first year and a half in America was the unhappiest period of his life. But a turn in his fortunes was at hand. . . .

The telegraph was then in its infancy. One line had been completed from the East to Pittsburgh, and its business was growing rapidly. David Brooks, the local manager, was a neighbor in Allegheny, and he and Uncle Tom Hogan enjoyed playing checkers with each other in the evenings.

One night they had just finished a game and were placing the checkers for another when Mr. Brooks said, "Our business is increasing so fast that we need another messenger boy—to deliver telegrams, you know. Do you happen to know of a good, thoroughly reliable boy that we can get?"

Mr. Hogan pondered a moment as he completed the placing of his men. Then, "I have a nephew who might do," he said. "Andrew Carnegie. He's as bright as a new dollar, honest and conscientious and not afraid of work."

"How old is he?"

Uncle Tom searched his memory and said, "Fourteen

19

and a half. He's small for his years, but smarter than his years. What will ye pay to such a lad?"

"Two and a half a week. If that's satisfactory, will you ask him to call at my office and talk it over?"

"I will."

No sooner had the two cronies ended their next game than Mr. Hogan strode over to the Carnegie home, where, though it was late in the evening, Mrs. Carnegie was still binding shoes. Uncle Tom's news produced a lively discussion. Andy's face shone with excitement. Oh, to get away from those bobbin vats! It seemed that the door to a new world was opening. But his father was doubtful.

"Mr. Brooks doesna know how small Andra is," he objected. "Judging by the wage that is offered, he is expecting a larger, stronger boy."

"I explained to him that Andy is small for his age but unusually bright," said Uncle Tom. "He isn't expecting a big fellow. I'm sure Andy will give satisfaction."

Mr. Carnegie shook his head. "Ye havena conseedered all the possibeelities, Tammas. He will be sent to all sorts of places, many of them where a boy shouldna go. He may be sent out on dark nights, perhaps into the country, with messages. And, to begin with, he doesna know the ceety—"

"I can learn it very quickly," put in Andrew, trembling with eagerness. "I will study it every moment—and I can take care of myself."

"No, na," said his father. "Ye'd better let well enough alone."

At that moment Andy's mother, who had been silently pondering the matter while she worked, delivered her judgment. "I think it would be a verra good thing for Andra," she said. "He canna be expected to work at that bobbin factory indefinitely. There's no opportunity for advancement there."

"Oh, and I do want to get away from it!" Andy's voice was choked with emotion. "I sometimes think I can't endure the stink of that oil a moment longer."

His father looked at him in surprise. He had not been aware of this revulsion.

"Why didn't ye tell us of this?" asked his mother.

"I didn't want to fret you."

"I think you should accept Mr. Brooks's offer," said his mother firmly.

"Mr. Brooks would like for him to call tomorrow," said Uncle Tom. "The telegraph office is at the corner of Fourth and Wood streets."

Andrew found it difficult to go to sleep that night, and he was awake early next morning.

At breakfast his father announced, "I will go with ye to see Mr. Brooks. But first I wish to consult Mr. Hay about it."

It seemed to Andy that Father was making much ado over a very simple matter. If it had been left to him, he would just have walked into Mr. Brooks's office and said, "I'll take the job." But so great was his reverence for his father that he said nothing, and Mr. Carnegie hurried off to consult Mr. Hay.

"It will be an inconvenience to me to lose him," said honest Mr. Hay, "but it will probably be an advantage to Andrew, and so I advise that he make the change. If the telegraph does not accept him, he may come back here."

Meanwhile Andy, in his best blue jacket and pantaloons, his face scrubbed and his ash-blond hair carefully combed, was being given final touches and inspection by his mother. It was a bright spring morning when he and his father walked the two miles to the telegraph office in Pittsburgh. They reached the corner of Fourth and Wood streets, and found that Mr. Brooks's office was on the second floor. At the door to the stairway Andrew acted on a resolution he had made on the way.

"Father," he said, halting and facing his father, "won't you stay here, please? Let me do this myself. Let me talk to Mr. Brooks alone." He did not add what he feared; namely, that his father would draw attention to his small stature and talk so disparagingly to Mr. Brooks that his chance of getting the job would be slim indeed. "Please, Father, I want to do this all my myself," he pleaded.

His father looked at him searchingly, then said, "Verra well, laddie. I'll wait here for ye." So he stood outside the entrance while Andrew went up to see the manager.

Mr. Brooks was so kindly that the boy was reassured at once. He tried to be fair in his sales talk.

"I don't know Pittsburgh well," said he, "but I can learn it very quickly. I know I'm small, and perhaps I shan't be strong enough for the place; but I believe I shall. All I ask is a trial."

"Is the wage—two and a half dollars a week—satisfactory?" asked the manager.

"Yes, sir, until I can earn more."

"When can you begin work?"

Andy needed no more than two seconds to decide that. "I can start now, if you wish."

"That's good," and then, raising his voice, "George!" he called.

A larger boy than Andy came from an adjoining room.

"George, this is our new messenger, Andrew Carnegie," said Mr. Brooks. "Andrew, George McLain will help you become acquainted with the city and our methods."

George was looking rather contemptuously at Andy. "What can we do with him?" he asked. "He's too small for his work."

"Let me be the judge of that," replied Mr. Brooks curtly. "Now take Andrew in there and get those telegrams from the operators. Let him go out with you today and see how you work."

Andy had spent some minutes with George in the operators' room before he remembered his father.

"My goodness!" he exclaimed. "I left my father standing
on the sidewalk. I must go down and tell him."

He ran down the stairs. "It's all settled, Father!" he cried.
"I've got the place, and I'm to begin work at once."

His beaming countenance was all that was needed to tell
his father how happy he was.

"I am glad for ye, laddie," he said, laying his hand on
the boy's shoulder. "Your mither will be gratified. I know
ye will do your best."

3

<hr />

The Messenger Boy

AS ANDREW LOOKED BACK UPON IT IN LATER YEARS, THAT day appeared as a milestone, a turning point, in his life. Now, freed from the dark cellar and the stinking oil vat, out in the sunlight and the bustle of the telegraph office and the city's streets, factories, and warehouses, Andy was happy and so full of the excitement of his work that he could scarcely eat his meals at home for telling the family about it. He set himself at once to learn the city, the pattern of its streets and the businesses in their order along them. He became acquainted with the prominent men of the city—merchants, business executives, professional men. One acquaintance of whom he was particularly proud was the attorney Edwin M. Stanton, who later became President Lincoln's Secretary of War.

As the business of the telegraph office increased, Mr.

Brooks spoke of the need for another boy. "I think I can get one for you, sir," said Andrew—and brought over from Allegheny a neighbor, David McCargo. George McLain departed, and one after another Andy provided from the ranks of the Bottom Hooshiers three more boys— Robert Pitcairn, Henry Oliver, and Willie Moreland. They took turns at reporting early enough in the morning to sweep out the office before business hours. When Superintendent Reid of the Eastern Telegraph Company, himself a Dunfermline man, visited Pittsburgh, he was so pleased with the squad of Scotch messenger boys that he put them into uniform—dark green jacket and trousers, a garb in which they attracted much attention on the streets of the city.

For delivering telegrams outside a certain limit, the messengers were permitted to collect an extra dime. Arguments arose among the boys, some charging the others with scheming to get more than their share of such deliveries. Ill feeling seemed to be developing, threatening their friendship, when Andy said to the group one morning, with characteristic diplomacy, "We mustn't go on like this. Let's not pay any attention to who delivers the messages. Let's put the dimes into a common fund and divide it equally among us at the end of the month."

He hadn't yet become familiar with the word "pool," as used in business; but that's what it was. The others pondered the proposal and agreed, specifying that Andy must be the treasurer. After that, there was no trouble except over the running accounts for candy and cakes, which the boys had been buying with their dimes and which they now bought on credit from a neighboring confectioner. Though some of them overdrew their accounts, the confectioner expected to be paid out of their monthly dividends—until Andy notified the merchant that he would not be responsible for debts contracted by the two or three overgreedy ones. Bob Pitcairn was the worst in his craving for sweets. When Andy scolded him for his extravagance, he declared solemnly, "I've got live things in my stomach, Andy, that gnaw my insides unless I feed 'em candy."

What a group of boys that was! Robert Pitcairn rose to the vice-presidency of the Pennsylvania Railroad, meanwhile investing on his own, and eventually became one of the wealthiest men in Pennsylvania. David McCargo also went in for railroads, building, among others, the Allegheny Valley Railway. Henry Oliver headed a great manufacturing concern, helped to develop the Minnesota iron-ore area, and died a multimillionaire. William Moreland prospered as a top-ranking attorney in Pittsburgh.

Andrew had been a messenger about a year when Mr. Glass, who ran the downstairs—the public—office, said to Mr. Brooks, "I'd like to have young Carnegie stay in the office a few minutes while I go out to attend to some business." So Andy, a little startled by this sudden call to higher duty, accepted telegrams to be sent, and saw that those which came from the operators' room were properly assigned to the messengers for delivery. After that he was frequently called to mind the office during the absences of Mr. Glass, who was beginning to dabble in politics.

By now the boys were being paid eleven dollars and a quarter a month. When the next pay day came and the messengers lined up to receive their wages, Andy, to his great consternation, was pushed aside while the other boys were being paid. His head whirled with panic. Was he about to be discharged? What could he have done that was wrong? But after the other boys had left the room, the manager confided to him that he had received a $2.25 raise in salary and handed him thirteen dollars and a half.

That was a Saturday evening. As Andy remembered it afterward, he ran most of the way home—ran on the wagon-way across the Allegheny bridge because the footway was so cluttered with pedestrians that he couldn't make the speed he desired. But en route he planned a dramatic stunt. As he reached Rebecca Street he slowed down to recover his breath . . . walked into the house and nonchalantly handed the usual eleven dollars and twenty-five cents to his mother. The other boys had always thought him stingy because he spent no money on himself; they did not know how close-knit the Carnegies were, how carefully the three earners of the family were hoarding their pennies to buy furniture and clothing and to pay off that loan of twenty pounds by their old friend, Mrs. Henderson, back in Scotland. . . .

Andy's mother was saving for this fund by stowing a silver half dollar, whenever she could spare it, in a stocking. When at last there were two hundred of these, Andy lugged them over to Pittsburgh; bought a draft for twenty pounds and sent it to Mrs. Henderson. It was a day of rejoicing; the Carnegie family was out of debt. . . .

But tonight Andy, though nearly bursting with his secret, said nothing of his good fortune until he and his nine-year-old brother, Tom, retired to their tiny bedroom in the attic. When he revealed his secret in a whisper and produced the two silver dollars and a twenty-five-cent piece from separate pockets—he had not wanted them to clink together and cause questions to be asked—Tom was almost too stunned by the magnificence of the event to speak. Finally he managed to ask, "What're you going to do with 'em, Andy?"

"Give 'em to Mother, of course!" replied Andy as he rolled into bed. "I just want to give the folks a big surprise. I'm on my way up now, Tom. Someday we'll go into business together—Carnegie Brothers."

"What kinda business?" Tom wanted to know.

"We-ell, I haven't decided yet; but we'll make our fortunes . . . and Father and Mother shall ride in their carriage." . . . He rambled on until a gentle snore apprised him that he had lost his audience.

At breakfast the next morning his parents could scarcely believe their eyes when he laid the two dollars and a quarter on the table. Tears welled into his mother's eyes, and his father, laying a hand on his shoulder, murmured, "Andra, I am proud of ye." He said late in life that no success or honor he ever attained had given him such a thrill as this simple triumph.

The messenger boys fully earned their wages. Every other evening they had to stay on duty until the office closed, and on those nights Andy seldom reached home before eleven o'clock. On alternate evenings they went off duty at six. It was a bitter pill, walking across that Allegheny bridge on blizzardy nights and mornings; but there could be no thought of paying for transportation.

There was one compensation for Andy on those evenings when he had to remain on duty. Not infrequently there were telegrams to be delivered to the manager of the Pittsburgh Theater, of whose magnificent interior Andy had often heard—the gilded scrollwork on the walls, the crimson velvet upholstery fastened with brass tacks, the great crystal chandeliers. One evening when he had a telegram to deliver to the theater, the genial manager let him go up to the top gallery, where seats were not reserved, and there he sat enthralled through a part of the play. After that, when he had a message for the theater manager near the end of the day, he contrived to delay delivering it until close to evening curtain time, which was earlier then than it is now.

Here the doors to a new world were opened for him. He had never read a line of Shakespeare in his life, and Shakespeare was one of the favorites among theater-goers in those days. Breathless with attention and suspense, the boy watched the gorgeous pageantry and ceremony and heard the immortal lines of the Bard of Avon spoken by Junius Brutus Booth, the Wallacks, Charlotte Cushman— all the eminent actors and actresses of the day. His retentive mind learned long passages from the plays before he ever saw them on paper. Thenceforth Shakespeare occupied a place in his esteem subordinate only to that of Burns and Scott.

Andy had read few books so far; for there was no public or circulating library in Pittsburgh or Allegheny, and the Carnegie family could spare no money for book buying. Colonel James Anderson, a retired manufacturer living in Allegheny, had accumulated a library of nearly four hundred volumes which he now proposed to share with working boys, such as he had once been. On Saturdays—the

Colonel himself acting as librarian—a boy might select a volume from the library and keep it until the following Saturday, when, if he returned it in good condition, he might borrow another. The plan became so popular that generous Colonel Anderson decided to enlarge upon it. He went to New York and bought more books until he had eighteen hundred, with which he proposed to establish "The Mechanics' and Apprentices' Library" if the city would provide a room for it. This the Council promptly agreed to do; a paid librarian was placed in charge and the work got under way.

But the new institution had a rule which was a blow to Andrew. It was free to regularly bound apprentices, but all others must pay two dollars a year for the privilege of drawing books. Andy visited the library and put a question to the librarian: "May a telegraph messenger boy draw books without charge?"

"Are you apprenticed?" asked the librarian.

"No, sir, but—"

"Messenger boys do not work with their hands," said the librarian with an air of finality.

"Perhaps not, but they do a lot of work with their legs," retorted Andy.

However, the librarian said that wasn't the same thing at all. Andy, much vexed, decided to make the matter public. So he wrote a letter which was printed in the

Pittsburgh Dispatch, complaining that, in restricting the use of the library to regularly articled apprentices, the new managers "have misunderstood the generous donor's intentions. It can hardly be thought that he meant to exclude boys employed in stores merely because they are not bound," and most of whom couldn't afford the two-dollar fee required. And he signed the letter "A working Boy, though not bound."

It was Andy's first venture into print and, when once he had had a taste of it, he took his pen in hand frequently thereafter. The librarian quickly replied, also through the newspaper columns, that it had been necessary to restrict the free list to "those for whose benefit the donation was made." As might be expected, Andy lost no time in retorting to this in another letter to the editor, in the course of which he said, "The question is, was the donation intended for the use of apprentices only in strict meaning of the word, viz., persons learning a trade and *bound,* or whether it was designed for working boys, whether bound or not? If the former is correct, then the managers have certainly misunderstood the generous donor's intentions. Working Boy."

The librarian must have consulted Colonel Anderson after the appearance of this note, for three days later, on the editorial page of the *Dispatch,* a line appeared, reading, " 'A Working Boy without a Trade' will confer a favor by calling at this office."

Andy called, was referred to the librarian and informed that the rule had been relaxed; all working boys, even though not apprenticed, were to be on the free list. So we owe Colonel James Anderson no small meed of gratitude for the idea behind the Carnegie free public libraries which have been such a blessing to the nation. Andrew Carnegie wrote in his later years: "To him I owe a taste for literature which I would not exchange for all the millions that were ever amassed by man." When he became wealthy, Carnegie erected a monument to the Colonel in front of the hall and library which he presented to Allegheny. The inscription thereon reads in part:

> To Colonel James Anderson, Founder of Free Libraries in Western Pennsylvania . . . This monument is erected in grateful remembrance by Andrew Carnegie, one of the "working boys" to whom were thus opened the precious treasures of knowledge and imagination through which youth may ascend.

With the exception of an occasional evening spent at Mr. Phipps's shoemaking shop with his cronies, John Phipps, Tom Miller, Jimmy Wilson, and Willie Cowley, Andy now occupied his evenings—those alternate evenings when he was at home—in reading Plutarch's *Lives;* the essays of Macaulay and Lamb; Prescott's histories of the Spanish conquests of Mexico and Peru; and especially Bancroft's *History of the United States,* which he read with closer attention than any other. But it is noteworthy that he also read very carefully some books on technical subjects, especially iron making—a forecast of his future, though of course nobody realized it then.

He kept up his correspondence with Uncle George Lauder and with young George, the beloved Cousin Dod of his childhood, and his letters—full of boasting about the freedom and enterprise of the United States—planted a seed in Cousin Dod's bosom which resulted a few years later in his emigrating to America.

William Carnegie had joined the Swedenborgian church and, though she remained aloof, his wife never interfered with his beliefs. Andy attended Sunday school there for several years, serving for a time as librarian of the little Sunday-school library—consisting mostly of books on Swedenborgian subjects—and writing occasional pieces for the Sunday-school paper, the *Dewdrop.* It is significant that one of these small essays was a protest against war, written when he was eighteen and during the first year of England's war against Russia in the Crimea. Andy also sang in the choir; he had a good ear, but the quality of his voice, as the leader confessed, left something to be desired. As usual, however, he found profit in the experience—a new interest in the Bach chorals which they frequently sang, and a developed appreciation of and taste for good music.

That his parents, though Scottish, were liberal in their thinking was proved one winter when the Allegheny River froze over, hard and smooth, on a Saturday. Remembering how strict most people in Scotland were about amusements on the Sabbath, Andy, who was very fond of skating, said with some hesitation to his parents that evening, "Would it be all right for me to skate awhile before church in the morning?"

"I think you may skate as long as you wish," promptly replied his broad-minded mother.

"I wouldna go so far as that, wife," amended his father. "I see no objection to your skating awhile in the morning, Andra; but I hope you will come home in time to go with me to church."

So Andy rose early and had some glorious hours on the frozen river.

Up the Ladder

ANDREW'S SERVICE AS A MESSENGER BOY LASTED A LITTLE
more than a year. He was fascinated from the very first
by the telegraph instruments and, when he had the opportunity, watched and listened closely to the operators as
they sent and received. He studied the Morse alphabet
and, on mornings when he came early to sweep out the
office, practiced on a disconnected instrument the quick,
sharp pressures for the dots and the long clicks that made
the dashes. He even ventured to call some neighboring
stations whose call letters he had learned, and which from
office gossip he knew were "manned" by boys in their
teens. Announcing himself as a learner, he passed a few
words back and forth with these fellows. One morning

when he was alone, he heard the call for Pittsburgh being given and repeated vigorously; and he ventured to answer. It was Philadelphia calling.

"I have an urgent message announcing a death," said Philadelphia. "Can you take it?"

"Yes," replied Andy.

The receiving instruments in those days printed the dots and dashes on a strip of paper. Andy copied the message and ran out to deliver it. He was somewhat worried over what Mr. Brooks would think of his presumption. "It was very urgent, sir," he apologized, "and I thought it best to handle it immediately."

"Quite right," said Mr. Brooks warmly. "You may do it whenever you are here alone. But"—he raised a finger warningly—"you must be very careful. We can't afford mistakes."

Not long after that the operators began leaving Andy in the office alone when they went out for lunch, and he not only accepted messages at the counter but even sent them. His pay was now raised to four dollars a week. Soon he found that by listening to the click of the instruments he could receive an incoming message, without having to rely on the dots and dashes embossed on the tape. So when he heard talk that a boy operator in Kentucky was creating quite a sensation by receiving messages entirely by ear, Andy could easily believe the reports.

An old chap named Hughes was the office copyist, reading the message from the tape and writing it out. He was disgruntled when Andy began operating, and muttered resentfully about being asked to copy "for a messenger boy." So Andy, just to show him what was what, stopped the reel of tape when a message came in, and began to take it by sound.

Hughes was scandalized. "You can't do that!" he protested. "It's never done."

"Jimmy Leonard, out in Kentucky, is doing it," retorted Andy, meanwhile listening and writing out the message. "It's easy."

"It will be a mess!" the old man insisted. "You will catch it for this."

But, instead, Andy's feat won him a promotion. The business of the office was rapidly increasing; another operator was needed, and Andy got the job at a salary of twenty-five dollars a month.

Not long afterward Mr. Brooks called Andrew to his desk and said, "Andy, you know where Greensburg is?"

"Yes, sir, east of here."

"Mr. Taylor, the operator there, wants to be off for a couple of weeks, and we will need someone to take his place. Do you think you can do the work?"

"Yes, sir," replied Andy without hesitation.

"Well, we'll send you there for a trial."

Great was the ado in the Carnegie household when Andy

brought the news. His mother was at once concerned about his wardrobe. "He must have a new shirt," she announced. But his father was astounded by the significance of the event.

"Think of the responsibeelity!" he exclaimed. "And he will not be seventeen until November. Do ye feel entirely competent, Andra, to cope with the task?"

"Yes, sir, I know I can do it," was the confident reply.

"Well, it is an honor which I am sure ye will be worthy of," declared his father.

The thirty-mile journey by stagecoach was a rare treat—especially the continuous pageant of workmen swarming all along the way, digging deep ruts and piling embankments for the Pennsylvania Railroad, which was pushing its line through from Philadelphia to Pittsburgh. Little did Andy dream that he was soon to be connected with that great enterprise.

The hotel in Greensburg was the first public house in which Andy had ever eaten a meal, and he thought the food wonderfully fine. Operator Taylor must have been considerably astonished when the smooth-faced, pink-cheeked, towheaded, undersized boy walked in and announced himself as the replacement. But he had communicated by wire with young Carnegie and knew something of his ability. As for Andrew, he was so anxious to do a good job that he stayed in the office until late in the evenings, so that no possible call might be missed. While sitting at his telegraph one evening during a thunderstorm—reading a book, of course—he ventured to touch the key just as lightning flashed. It was as if a giant had struck him with a spiked club—he found himself and his stool sprawled on the floor, his nerves tingling. After this startling lesson he was extremely cautious during storms.

Andy became something of a celebrity in Greensburg; people visited the office just to see him receive messages by ear. He completed his chore there with great credit and, after his return to Pittsburgh, Mr. McCalla, the manager of the Eastern Telegraph Company, sent him as a token of appreciation a beautifully bound copy of Burns's poems. Nothing could have pleased him more.

Each of the five Pittsburgh newspapers had been in the habit of sending a reporter to the telegraph office to get the Eastern and foreign news, but now they decided to pool their interests and send only one. At this reporter's suggestion Andy made five copies of all such news items, for which he received a dollar a week—thus raising his monthly income to nearly thirty dollars.

The Carnegie family now felt sufficiently strong financially to cease paying rent and buy a home. Uncle Andrew Hogan's cottage and lot on Rebecca Street could be had for five hundred and fifty dollars, with two years in which to pay, and they took it over.

Andy was seventeen and a half when a spring flood in the Ohio washed out the twenty-five-mile stretch of wire between Steubenville and Wheeling, cutting off a part of the Middle West from communication with the East. Andrew was sent to Steubenville to maintain the connection until the wires could be restrung. Receiving the messages from the East, he sent them at intervals of an hour or so by small boats down the river to Wheeling. On their return the boats brought packages of telegrams from Columbus, Cincinnati, Louisville, St. Louis, and other places; Andy wired these messages, thus maintaining uninterrupted service for more than a week.

While he was there, he received a letter from his father informing him that he would be coming down the river on a certain day with some tablecloths which he hoped to sell in Wheeling and Cincinnati. Andy was at the wharf when the boat arrived and had to look about awhile before he saw his father beckoning him to come aboard. William led the way to a nook on the lower deck among the freight.

"I didna like to go far from my bundles," he explained, "for fear of theft."

"Haven't you a cabin?" asked his son in consternation.

"No, I thought I must economize; so I'm taking deck passage."

"Oh, Father!" Andy's voice choked on the words.

"It's really not bad," protested his father. "I have my

42

blanket, ye see, and I think I shall sleep verra weel. Sales may not be easy, ye know, son, and I must be careful."

"Well, Father," burst out Andy, "it will not be long before Mother and you shall ride in your carriage."

His father grasped his hand silently, but his eyes were wet. And when, a quarter of an hour later, the boat was about to depart, William gave his boy's hand another fervent squeeze and murmured, "Andra, I am proud of ye!"

Thomas A. Scott, a remarkable man, was superintendent of the Pittsburgh Division of the Pennsylvania Railroad at this time. He came occasionally to the telegraph office to exchange messages with his superior, General Superintendent Lombaert, at Altoona. On these visits he eyed the young operator and often stayed to talk with him.

One day one of Mr. Scott's assistants came in with a telegram and said to Andy, "Mr. Scott was talking about you this morning."

"Is that so? What did he say?" Andy was alert at once.

"He asked if I thought he could get you as his clerk and operator. The road is going to have its own telegraph, you see. I told him it was impossible; that you are well satisfied in your present job—"

"Hold on! Not so fast!" interrupted Andy, with uplifted hand. "He can have me if he wants me. Go and tell him so."

The result was that on February 1, 1853, Andrew went to work for Mr. Scott at a salary of $35 a month. Promotions were coming so rapidly that he was somewhat awed by them.

Now his mother could stop binding shoes . . . and soon he was able to place David McCargo and Robert Pitcairn in jobs with the railroad. Bob became assistant to General Superintendent Lombaert at Altoona, then only a village but potentially the great nerve center of the Pennsylvania system. . . .

Andy went to Altoona monthly to get the cash for the Pittsburgh payroll, and on his second trip the dour, taciturn general superintendent astonished him by inviting him home for tea. At the door Mr. Lombaert introduced the guest to Mrs. Lombaert with "This is Mr. Scott's Andy" and, in his own home, proved to be not nearly so cold as he had seemed in the office. Andy admired Mr. Scott so much that he was quite content with the label bestowed upon him. One day J. Edgar Thomson, president of the railroad, came to the office in Pittsburgh, thrust his head into the young assistant's room and asked, "Are you Mr. Scott's Andy?" It came to be a common designation for him.

One morning Andy reached the office to find that an accident on the Eastern Division had delayed the westbound express and that the eastbound passenger trains were creeping along, sending out a flagman at every curve, while freight trains in both directions were standing still on sidings. On single-track railroads the system of train operation was still very primitive.

No one knew where Mr. Scott was . . . perhaps he had been called away on business. . . . Andy was so worried over the situation that he could not resist the temptation to straighten it out and give the overworked trainmen some respite from strain. He had handled similar emergencies before under Mr. Scott's direction; so now he began dispatching trains, naming meeting points, on his own responsibility, and had everything running smoothly when at last the super reached the office.

Hurrying to Andy's desk, he asked, "Well, how are matters?"

Andy's voice almost failed him as he replied, "Mr. Scott, I could not find you anywhere and I gave these orders in your name early this morning."

He displayed copies of the orders and gave the present position of every train on the line, freight and passenger. At the end the superintendent looked rather wonderingly into Andy's face; but he said nothing and went to his own room, leaving the boy still in suspense as to how his daring action would be regarded. Not until the next day were his overstrung nerves relieved, when Mr. Franciscus, the freight agent, told him with a chuckle what Mr. Scott had said to him: "Do you know what that little white-haired Scotch devil of mine did?"

45

"No."

"I'm darned if he didn't run every train on the division in my name without the slightest authority."

"And did he do it all right?"

"Oh, yes—all right." And that was that.

Thereafter Mr. Scott turned over more and more responsibility to Andy. Once he was absent for ten days and, with Mr. Lombaert's approval, left his young clerk in full charge of the division—a remarkable trust for a youth in his twentieth year. During his incumbency there was a small wreck —that of a construction train—and Andy was very severe with the men whose negligence had brought it about; he discharged the chief offender and suspended two others. When Mr. Scott returned, Andy gathered from him that he had been too harsh; and his remorse was great and lasting —he tried to make amends in one way or another to the men whom he had treated so rigorously.

In the fall of 1855—before they had fully paid for their own home—William Carnegie died, after a short illness, at the age of fifty—"just as we were becoming able to give him leisure and comfort," said Andy. The family was overwhelmed with grief by the passing of the gentle, modest father who, as his elder son always maintained, was the finest, most lovable man he had ever known.

His illness and death threw an additional financial burden on Andrew and his mother, and the latter went back to her shoe-binding. Such was the situation when Mr. Scott said one day, "Andy, have you five hundred dollars to spare?"

Andy's salary had been raised to forty dollars a month and, as he handled the payroll, he always drew it in the form of two golden double-eagles, which seemed to him "the prettiest works of art in the world." But they always melted away quickly under the exigencies of the moment, and it occurred to Andy when his boss asked that question that he hadn't even five hundred cents to spare.

Before he could think of an answer, however, Mr. Scott, ignoring with a twinkle his young assistant's startled look, went on, "Because, if you have, I know of an investment for you: ten shares of Adams Express Company stock, one of the best on the market—positively gilt-edged; pays a monthly dividend of one dollar a share. A man I know is forced to raise cash quickly, and so must let this stock go. Can you get the money?"

Andy's head was buzzing as he tried to think where on earth he might lay hands on five hundred dollars. He mustn't miss this chance, especially when his kindly chief, instead of grabbing the bargain himself, was making a sacrifice to give it to him.

"I think I can manage it somehow, sir," said he.

Five hundred dollars had been paid on the Rebecca Street home, and Andy hoped it might be possible to pledge

that for a loan of the full amount. There was only one person who would possibly take such a risk. Andy's mother,
with full confidence in Mr. Scott's judgment, said, "I will
ask Brother William for the money." She took a fifty-mile
steamboat journey down the Ohio to East Liverpool, where
William Morrison had become a person of substance—a justice of the peace and a sort of investment broker for the
farmers in the neighborhood. He provided the money, taking a second mortgage on the home, and his sister returned
to Pittsburgh in triumph.

Several days had elapsed, however, before Andrew was
able to deliver the cash to Mr. Scott; and when he did, he
was met by unexpected news. "That man Reynolds has
stiffened his price for the stock. He wants six hundred
now."

Andrew was stunned for a moment, but Mr. Scott added,
"I'll take care of the extra hundred for the present. You can
pay me when and as it is convenient."

The days went on, and one morning an envelope of heavy
white paper bearing the corner medallion of the Adams
Express Company lay on Andy's desk. It was addressed in
a big, slashing script to "Andrew Carnegie, Esq.," and in-
side was a check on the Gold Exchange Bank of New York
for ten dollars—his first monthly dividend. To the end of
his life he never forgot that big, flourishing signature of
"J. C. Babcock, Cashier," or the thrill of receiving his first

revenue from capital investment—something he had not worked and sweated for with his hands. "Eureka!" he whispered to himself. "Here is the goose that lays the golden eggs."

He saved that check over the week end and showed it to four chums—Tom Miller, John Phipps, Jimmy Wilson, and Willie Cowles—as they were enjoying a ramble in the woods. They made great sport of that "Esquire" attached to his name, but they were tremendously impressed, nevertheless, by the dividend check.

"This is the way to get ahead," said John Phipps.

"You're right, John," agreed Jimmy Wilson. "I'm going to keep an eye out for opportunities like this."

"Let's all do it"—Tom Miller was enthusiastic—"and keep each other informed."

"And if one of us hears of something—some investment that's too big for him—let's all go into it together, if we can," said Andrew.

"A great idea," approved Tom. And so they did for several years thereafter, whenever it was practicable.

That quintet had some lively debates of evenings in Mr. Phipps's shoemaking shop after his few journeymen had gone home—debates always on current problems, with Andy, the extreme proletarian, enthusiastically in favor of letting the people pass on every question. He once orated for an hour and a half—at least, so Tom Miller claimed afterward—in favor of the election of all judges by popular vote, a stand the impracticability of which he came to realize in later years. There is no telling how much longer he might have talked on the subject had not a messenger entered breathlessly and said, "Mr. Carnegie, you're wanted. There's a wreck at Derry"—at which he clapped on his hat and coat; said, "Some of you tell my family where I've gone"; and vanished, running.

Eventually the five of them joined the Webster Literary Society, the foremost club of its kind in the city, and were proud of being considered worthy of membership.

In his younger days Andrew had aspirations toward journalism; he thought he would particularly have liked to be an editor. He had written a letter on a public topic to the *New York Tribune* a few years ago, and now he wrote one to the *Pittsburgh Dispatch* criticizing the inhospitable attitude of that city toward the Pennsylvania Railroad. The letter was published anonymously, but Mr. Stokes, chief counsel for the railroad company, persuaded the editors to tell him the writer's name. As a result, he invited the author to his home at Greensburg for a week end. Andrew accepted hesitantly, doubting that he could do or say anything likely to interest so brilliant and educated a man as Mr. Stokes—in which surmise he was wrong.

Here he spent his first night as a guest in a strange house. He was deeply impressed by what he considered the magnificence of the Stokes residence, and especially by a marble mantel in the library. Carven in the center of the arch was the representation of an open book, with the inscription:

> He that cannot reason is a fool;
> He that will not, a bigot;
> He that dare not, a slave.

As Andy stared at the beautiful structure, his soul stirred under the impact of the blunt lines. "Someday," he said to himself, "someday I'm going to have a library, and those words shall be cut in the mantel." And in the course of time they were cut in two mantels—in the Carnegie homes in New York and Scotland.

He was now being invited out more and more, and thereby receiving some much-needed object lessons in the correct social usages of the day. Mrs. Franciscus, wife of the general freight agent, was very hospitable to him, though he was so shy that it was a long time before she could persuade him to eat a meal at her home.

In 1856 Mr. Scott succeeded Lombaert as general superintendent and had to move his office to Altoona, taking Andy with him; and of course his mother and Tom went with Andrew. Mrs. Carnegie had again ceased her shoe-binding, and now, when they had succeeded in renting a pleasant cottage in Altoona, Andrew decreed that she must have a servant.

"You've worked hard all your life, and now it's time for you to begin taking things more easily," he told her.

The explosion that followed was even worse than he had expected.

"What! Have a strange woman in my hoose, making free with everything!" she exclaimed. "That I will not! I've kept hoose for my boys all these years, cooked for ye, washed and mended your clothes, and now ye ask me to sit down and fold my hands; ye put me on the shelf; I'll na endure it, laddie. No woman will know how to cook the food you boys like—"

"Dear Mother," pleaded Andy, when he could get a word in edgewise, "you have done everything for Tom and me; you've been everything to us. Now let us do something for you; let us be partners and always think what is best for each other. The time has come for you to play the lady. Someday soon you are to ride in your carriage. Meanwhile, do get that girl in to help you. Tom and I would like this."

She finally consented, though only after much grumbling. After the servant came, she began to go about among the elders of such society as Altoona afforded. Self-educated, she had the poise and natural refinement necessary to carry her through any eventuality; and she began to enjoy the new phase of her life, which included gardening and flowers.

Mr. Scott, whose wife had died a short time ago, had brought his niece, Miss Rebecca Stewart, to preside over his home. A fine young woman, a few years older than Andrew, she played the part of elder sister to him, quietly giving him some hints on social usage which he needed. They went for long drives through the hills, and she invited him to the house for dinner now and then. On one such occasion Tom Miller, now a rising young railroad man, was another guest. Mr. Scott was out of town. While they sat at table—both Miss Stewart and the maid were out of the room for a moment—Andrew, not yet accustomed to the wonder of the life he was leading, picked up the cream pitcher reverently and murmured, "Real silver, Tom!"

5

The Rolling Snowball

A SUIT WAS BROUGHT AGAINST THE RAILROAD IN WHICH MR. Stokes suspected that Andrew would be subpoenaed as a witness. Needing more time for preparation, he desired a postponement of the trial; so he asked Manager Scott to hustle his young assistant out of the state for a short while. Andrew accordingly journeyed to Crestline, Ohio, where he spent several days visiting with Tom Miller and Jimmy Wilson, both railroaders there. They were saddened by the recent death of John Phipps by a fall from a horse—the first break in a circle of youth wholly unprepared for such a catastrophe. John's younger brother Henry, as time went on, became very dear to Andy, and a partner in some of his enterprises.

While Andy was riding through Ohio in a coach en route to Crestline, he was approached by a rustic-looking man carrying a green bag. "The brakeman tells me you are connected with the Pennsylvania Railroad," he said.

"Yes, sir, I am," was the reply.

"My name is Theodore Woodruff," said the stranger. "I have here a model of a car for night traveling—my own invention. May I show it to you?"

"Certainly."

Mr. Woodruff took the model from his bag—a portion of a sleeping car. It had rows of seats on each side in pairs, two seats facing each other, which at night could, by means of a connecting spring pad and a thin mattress, be made into a bed. Above the windows was another bed which, though cleverly concealed in the wall during the daytime, could be let down at night, supported by chains; when not being slept in, it was a storage space for the mattresses and bedclothes. In short, it was in practically all its details the Pullman sleeping car we have known from 1870 to the present day.

There had been a few so-called sleeping cars on the railroads for nearly twenty years; but self-respecting men abhorred trying to sleep in them, and no woman ever did. They were little better than boxcars with two or three tiers of shelves along each side, and the passengers lay upon these shelves—usually with their clothes on, though some did go so far as to take off their boots.

The proposed Woodruff car was quite a different matter.

As Andrew examined the model, his excitement rose; he told himself that here was something that would revolutionize traveling. He asked many questions.

"It is only fair to tell you," said Woodruff, "that my idea has been given a halfhearted trial by the New York Central, though under very unfavorable conditions. It didn't have a fair chance."

"Would you come to Altoona if I send for you?" asked Andrew.

"To be sure I would."

"Well, I'll lay the matter before Mr. Scott as soon as I get back. Give me your address."

That sleeping car haunted Andrew throughout his stay in Ohio. When he returned to Altoona, he burst into Scott's office and, without asking about the lawsuit, exclaimed, "Mr. Scott, I've got hold of a great idea—a car in which you can really go to bed and sleep at night!"

The manager leaned back with a half smile on his face as he listened. He was accustomed to the boy's enthusiasms, but he was also aware that they usually had a solid foundation. "You certainly believe in this thing, young man," said he. "All right, tell your friend to bring his model over and I'll look at it."

When Woodruff, notified by telegraph, came to Altoona, Scott was deeply impressed by his model. "What is your proposition?" he asked.

"That your company build the cars and operate them, paying me a royalty," replied the inventor.

Details were discussed, and Mr. Scott decided to have two of the cars built at once. Andrew walked out with Mr. Woodruff, and was greatly surprised when the inventor turned to him in the outer office and said, "Mr. Carnegie, would you like to come in with me on this business?"

Andrew was momentarily startled into silence. He had little or no ready cash, but here was another of those opportunities—like that of the Adams Express stock—to set a stream of dividends rolling in his direction, and it mustn't be missed.

"Perhaps I would," he said. "Just how do you mean?"

"I was thinking of letting you buy an eighth interest in my company—which I am going to organize right away."

He named figures, and Andrew admitted his lack of ready money. After some discussion Woodruff suggested that he pay for the stock by installments. The first installment would be $217.50, and Andrew had no means of getting it but by borrowing. He went to the local banker, Mr. Lloyd—a big, genial six-footer who knew and liked him— and asked if he might have the money for investment purposes.

"Sure it's a good investment?" queried the banker, putting his massive arm across his young friend's shoulders.

"Yes, sir, it's in a sleeping-car company. Our railroad is

about to begin building two of the cars on a royalty basis."

"Of course I'll lend you the money," said Mr. Lloyd. "You're a good risk, Andy."

So, for the first time in his life, he signed a promissory note to a bank, and made the payment on the stock. Ever afterward he thought of that event as the beginning of his fortune. The dividends soon began to take care of the installment payments on his stock. The Pennsylvania built other sleepers, and so did other roads. By the time he was twenty-five years old his income from his sleeping-car stock was $5000 a year. "In the words of Sancho Panza," he remarked, "blessings light on him that first invented sleep."

The Carnegies had been in Altoona three years when one day in the autumn of 1859 Mr. Scott said to his assistant, "Andy, they are thinking of making me vice-president of the railroad company. I am going to Philadelphia next week to discuss the matter with Mr. Thomson."

Andrew was depressed by the news. When his admired, almost idealized chief was snatched away to Philadelphia, what would be the effect upon himself? So far he had no standing save as an appendage to Mr. Scott. Would the boss find a job for him in Philadelphia? He fervently hoped so; he dreaded the thought of working under anyone else.

When the manager returned from his trip, he called Andy into his office.

"It's all settled," said he. "As vice-president, I am to be removed to Philadelphia. Mr. Lewis will be my successor as general manager."

As he talked on, Andrew's nerve tension increased.

"Now about yourself," said the boss at last, "Mr. Potts"— superintendent of the Pittsburgh Division—"is to be promoted to the transportation department in Philadelphia, and I recommended you to the president as his successor. Do you think you could handle the Western Division?"

Andrew's head swam for only a moment. Success and advancement had built up his self-confidence almost to the point of cocksureness. His twenty-fourth birthday was still a few days off. . . . He thought of what was being said of Lord John Russell—that, although he was only a politician and a landlubber, he would take command of the Channel Fleet tomorrow, if asked. So would Wallace or Bruce. . . .

"Yes, sir, I think I can," Andy replied, but with the implication, "I know I can."

"Well, Mr. Thomson has agreed to give you a trial at it," Scott went on. "What salary do you think you ought to have?"

"Salary!" exclaimed the new super. It hadn't entered his head. "It isn't the salary I'm interested in," he said loftily. "It's the position I want. It will be glory enough to take over the Pittsburgh Division in your former place. You may

59

make my salary whatever you please—what I'm getting now, if you like."

(That was sixty-five dollars a month.)

Mr. Scott refrained from smiling at his naïveté. "When I was on that job," he said, "I drew fifteen hundred a year. Mr. Potts is getting eighteen hundred. I think it would be right to start you at fifteen hundred, and after a while, if you succeed, you will get the raise to eighteen hundred. Would that be satisfactory?"

A nod and a wave of the hand signified that this was a minor matter to the new official.

Once more he hurried home, eager to tell of his good fortune. He wanted to run, but that would have been beneath the dignity of the superintendent of the Pittsburgh Division of the Pennsylvania Railroad. His mother was only briefly overwhelmed by the news. After all, it was no more than was to be expected from a boy like Andra. And now she was confronted with the problem of moving back to Pittsburgh. "It will be pleasant to get back among old friends and kin," she said, "but I dread the soot."

"Now, Tom," said Andrew to his sixteen-year-old brother, "how would you like to be my secretary?"

"Fine!" exclaimed Tom. He had become an expert telegrapher, and a division superintendent had many messages to send and receive by wire.

Andrew tried not to be too hoity-toity when he seated

himself at the superintendent's desk and began giving orders. He suspected that some of the older employees were grumbling among themselves about the little upstart who had somehow wormed his way into this high-level job; it made him all the more determined to prove that, despite his size, he was big enough to fill the place. He had plenty of opportunities that winter to prove his quality. The division superintendent was expected to be on the job day and night when there was trouble. If an accident occurred at night, he was notified at once and went to the scene to supervise the clearing up.

And what a tough winter that was! Cast-iron "chairs" were used in those days to grip the rails to the ties and, in very cold weather, cast iron becomes brittle and breaks easily. That winter there was an almost constant succession of breaks and derailings. In one bitter night alone no fewer than forty-seven of those chairs broke, at one place and another. The new super during that cold spell was away from home for eight days on end, visiting wrecks and simple derailments.

It occurred to him afterward that he had probably been an inconsiderate taskmaster, for he never knew fatigue himself; he had the rare gift of being able to lie down on the floor of a boxcar, or anywhere else, and fall asleep immediately, regardless of the uproar around him—and, no matter how short the nap, he always awoke refreshed. Besides, he was fired with the zeal of a conscientious and ambitious young man eager to make good in a new and responsible position.

Sure enough, the smoke and soot of Pittsburgh had been a shock when they returned to it. "It's worse than it used to be," they told one another—and it might be added that it was worse then than it is now. Margaret Carnegie's housewifely soul was in despair over the impossibility of keeping anything clean.

"I wish we could live in the country," said Andrew at the office one day.

"Well, why don't you?" retorted D. A. Stewart, general freight agent for the railroad and a nephew of Mr. Scott. "Come out to Homewood. There's a place that can be bought right now, adjoining mine. Beautiful situation, not too far out; only about a dozen families in the neighborhood, all top grade. I'll get an option on that property for you if you like, until you can go out and look it over."

Andrew and his mother went to inspect the place and were delighted with it. It was a two-story cottage embowered in trees—in a village of extensive lawns, woods, and glens, with a little creek rippling through it. The Carnegie home was one of the smaller ones in the town, but there was plenty of room for the family. Here Margaret spent some of the happiest years of her life, extending her circle

of friendships and cultivating an even larger flower garden
than she had had in Altoona.

And a telegraph wire was run into the house, so that the
young super could remain on call in case of trouble at any
hour of the night or Sunday.

Their neighbors the Stewarts grew increasingly dear to
them. Mr. Stewart eventually became a partner in the
Carnegie iron and steel business, as did another and
younger neighbor, John Vandevort, whom Andrew here
met for the first time. Beloved "Vandy" was a traveling
companion on some of Andrew's later trips abroad. And the
Carnegie migration to Homewood brought at least one
other settler there—that tried and true friend, congenial in
his love of music, books, and travel, Thomas N. Miller. One
of Andrew Carnegie's endearing traits was his capacity for
friendship. His loyalty to friends was intense and lasting;
he never forgot. Some of the happiest days in his declining
years were those when he again encountered, after long
separation, friends of his youth.

He was taken wholeheartedly into the intellectual, cul-
tured society of Homewood. The great man of the suburb
was the elderly scholar Judge William Wilkins, who, though
now retired, had been Senator, Secretary of War, and Minister to Russia; his wife came from a family of statesmen
and diplomats, and was a distant kinswoman of the poet
Byron. This awe-inspiring acquaintanceship, as well as that

with a Mrs. Addison and her daughter Leila, gave Andrew's self-satisfaction a jolt and, as he confessed later in life, made him realize "the indescribable and immeasurable gulf that separated the highly educated from people like myself." The conversations around the fire in Judge Wilkins's drawing room set him to reading Darwin and Herbert Spencer and John Stuart Mill, and his contacts with Miss Addison smoothed away some of the rough edges still remaining in his speech and manner.

In the "West"—where Pittsburgh and the vicinity were still considered to be—young men affected a rough carelessness in dress, going in for loose collars and heavy boots. Anything that could be labeled as foppish was held in contempt. A minor official of the railroad who wore kid gloves at times was an object of derision. Young Carnegie had such notions gently taken out of him by Miss Addison, who also curbed—a little—his assertiveness, which came dangerously near to arrogance. He was never a snob—never ashamed of his humble beginnings or, oddly enough, of his need for polish and improvement. Despite his self-assurance, there was an honesty, a frankness, and a naïveté about him which made him likeable and popular.

Another neighbor was William Coleman, one of Pittsburgh's wealthy citizens, an ironmaster and patron of the arts, long proprietor of the Pittsburgh Opera House. But for the young fellows of Homewood and Pittsburgh, Mr. Cole-

man's chief asset consisted of five charming daughters—
two of whom, by the way, eventually became the wives of
Thomas N. Miller and Thomas M. Carnegie respectively.

After oil was discovered in northwestern Pennsylvania in
1859, Mr. Coleman and Andrew went on a scouting expe-
dition up the Allegheny Valley. They knocked about in the
rough backwoods country for days, sleeping and eating
when and as they could. Prospectors at that time were not
displaying such madness as appeared during later oil booms,
and all thinking and doing were in comparatively smaller
figures—which explains why Mr. Coleman and Andrew
were able, after some chaffering, to buy outright for forty
thousand dollars a farm which seemed to lie near enough
to proven territory to be a good gamble. Scotchman though
he was, Andrew Carnegie was not afraid to risk on new
ventures. His belief in his own ability, and his steady ascent
toward success, had given him an unconscious confidence
in his destiny—and all contributed to his willingness to
take a chance.

The man who sold that farm was probably well satisfied
with his deal—at the time. The buyers were taking all the
risk, and had given him enough money to make him comfortable for the rest of his life. But when, three or four
years later—with a dozen or more wells on the place spout-
ing that rich, black Pennsylvania petroleum—the value of
the property was roughly estimated to be five million dol-

lars, the former owner must have suffered some acute heart-burnings.

It was largely a Homewood group who, as owners of that farm, organized the Columbia Oil Company—Coleman (with a large slice of course), Carnegie, Vandevort, Tom Miller, and others. Even teen-age Tom Carnegie was put into it for a modest share by his elder brother, who advanced the money.

That was indeed the golden age of Opportunity, for those who had the nerve and quick wit to answer her knock at the door. Thereafter Andrew Carnegie did not lack money for investment. He bought more Adams Express and Woodruff stock and began buying into Western Union Telegraph. His fortune, like a rolling snowball, accumulated the more rapidly as it grew larger.

6

‖‖

Bull Run and Dunfermline

FOR SOME TIME PAST, YOUNG CARNEGIE, ALWAYS KEENLY
interested in and observant of national events and problems, had been deeply concerned over the growing rift
between the North and the South over the questions of
slavery and states' rights. He could not believe that his
beloved nation was about to be wrecked upon political
shoals; indeed he was so profoundly stirred by the crisis
that he became what President Cleveland later called an
"offensive partisan." In the early spring of 1861, when the
Southern states were seceding as the result of the election
of President Lincoln, he spent a Sunday at the home of his
good friend Mr. Stokes at Greensburg and was shocked to
hear his host assert that the Federal government had no
right to use force to prevent secession.

"Mr. Stokes," flashed Andrew, "we'll be hanging men
like you in less than six weeks!"

To his discomfiture Mr. Stokes burst into laughter.

"Nancy!" he called to his wife in an adjoining room. "Nancy, listen to this young Scotch demon. He says they'll be hanging men like me in less than six weeks!"

But within six weeks Mr. Stokes was a major in the Federal army. His talk against the use of force to curb secession was just that of a stanch Democrat against the Republican administration. He had regarded the affair as a mere partisan wrangle—until the firing on Fort Sumter shocked him into a realization that this was war. There were many like him who did not at first comprehend the seriousness of the break.

War service came quickly for Pennsylvania Railroad men. Scott was made Assistant Secretary of War in charge of the Transportation Department; and he promptly summoned his "young reliable," Andrew Carnegie, to act as his aide in charge of the military railroads and telegraphs, and to organize a force of railway men. The first southbound troops from Massachusetts had been attacked by a mob while passing through Baltimore, and the rail line south of that city had been cut in several places by burned bridges and torn-up track. For a week after April 19, communication between Washington and the North was broken —a very dangerous situation.

Carnegie's first job was to restore that track. Again he drove relentlessly a force of engineers, tracklayers, and men snatched from the regiments awaiting transportation, and at the end of a week the trains began to move slowly southward. Leaving his men to reballast the roadbeds and to strengthen the track for the heavier service which it must bear thereafter, he went toward Washington in the engine cab of the first trainload of troops to pass over the repaired road. They were moving cautiously, for fear of further sabotage, and were still several miles from Washington when Andrew noticed that the single telegraph wire had been loosened from the poles and pinned down to the ground by stakes.

"Stop here!" he said to the engineer. "I want to release that telegraph wire."

"Has it been cut?" asked the engineer as he shut off steam and reversed his locomotive, for there was as yet no air brake.

"No," replied Andrew. "It seems to have been just pegged down to the earth for some reason. Even hanging in a festoon, it will work—which it won't do when it's grounded like this."

He dropped from the cab, ran to the peg and, using both hands and all his strength, pulled it out of the ground. He had not thought of what would happen when the taut wire was suddenly released. It whipped upward—striking him in the face, knocking him down, and cutting a gash across his cheek which bled profusely. And thus he went into Washington with the troops, holding a bloody handkerchief to his face. He boasted humorously that he was among the first to shed his blood for the Union in the Civil War.

Reaching Washington, he found the War Department short of telegraphers and was ordered to find four more for war service. He repeated the order by wire to his old boyhood friend David McCargo, now the superintendent of telegraphs for the Pennsylvania Railroad. Within an hour McCargo replied, naming four operators from various stations along the line who would be leaving for Washington at once. Their ages ranged from eighteen to twenty-three, and the eldest of them, Strouse, became the government's superintendent of telegraphs!

Carnegie's next duty was to re-establish communication—which had been severed—across the Potomac River and into Virginia, to enable a Federal army to move into that area for the defense of the capital. The old Long Bridge across the Potomac had to be rebuilt—with wood, of course —and that was accomplished in a week with everybody, the boss included, working round the clock. All told, the young super spent six weeks in repairing damages to tracks, bridges, and telegraph lines and in building new ones. That summer of 1861 was unusually hot, and one day Carnegie, fatigued by incessant work, suffered a slight sunstroke. Thereafter, until the end of his life, the hot summers of America were oppressive to him and he had to be careful not to spend too much time in the sun.

On the day of the Battle of Bull Run, July 21—the battle which was such an eye opener to the Union—Carnegie was at Burke's Station, twenty miles from Washington, moving troops, munitions, and supplies to the front by rail. Over-confidence reigned in the capital; it was the official opinion that the presumptuous Southerners would be easily de-feated, and the little uprising quickly brought to an end.

At Burke's, Carnegie had a strenuous day. Ambulances were bringing in the wounded in increasing numbers, keep-ing him busy getting engines and cars from Washington to carry the patients back to the hospitals in and around the city. The early news from the field was optimistic. But by mid-afternoon an ominous change in the situation began to be evident; retreating soldiers were streaming past the Station, some in units, many as stragglers. It rapidly be-came clear that, instead of a great victory, there had been a great disaster. Trainload after trainload of wounded were sent back, and the wagon roads were choked with retreat-ing troops and the carriages of Congressmen and officials who had driven out, some of them with their families, to witness the triumph. Dusk approached as the terrible rout went on. The sound of firing was very near when Carnegie boarded a train for Washington. Thereafter he was in the capital for several weeks, and made the acquaintance of many of the top men in government and the army. These included President Lincoln, who was his usual frank, af-fable self with Carnegie and made a profound impression on him.

Official Washington at first believed that the war was a mere flare-up which would be over in a few weeks, and so railroad men such as Scott and Carnegie had been rushed in only for the emergency. The stunning setback at Bull Run changed all official thinking. It was now seen that the war might drag on for a year or two or three, and Scott and Carnegie could not remain away from their railroad posts for so long. As well-run railroads—particularly such an important one as the Pennsylvania—were necessary to the successful prosecution of the war, Scott and Carnegie went back to their jobs, and permanent appointees took over the government rail and telegraph work.

Back in Pittsburgh, Carnegie picked up the threads of his work but continued—as most ambitious officials did then—to develop outside interests and investments.

Near the end of the following winter he was seriously ill for several weeks, and when he returned to his office he still felt so enervated that he asked for a leave of absence in order to recuperate. It was granted—three months of it!—and there was no question in Carnegie's mind as to where he would spend the vacation. Late in May he wrote to young George Lauder—cousin "Dod"—that he and his mother were coming to Dunfermline for a visit.

When they sailed for Liverpool, on June 28, they were accompanied by the inseparable Tom Miller, who was bound for a ramble through Britain. Andrew and his mother were keyed up to a high pitch of happy excitement as the train sped northward from Liverpool, threaded the Cheviot Hills, and entered Scotland. At the first sight of a hillside covered with a mass of rippling yellow flowers, Margaret Carnegie murmured, "Oh, there's the broom! The broom!" —and her tears overflowed. As for her son, "I felt as if I could throw myself upon the sacred soil and kiss it," he said afterward.

At Dunfermline they were welcomed heartily by the numerous kinsfolk, who competed for the honor of entertaining them. Mrs. Carnegie stopped with her own family, the Morrisons, while Andrew went straight to the apartment of Uncle George Lauder, over his grocery shop, where the two younger men were still "Dod" and "Naig" to each other, as they had been in boyhood. One evening early in the visit the three of them ranted through a scene from *Douglas,* a bombastic old eighteenth-century tragedy, just as they had done when Dod and Naig were boys, and found that they were still almost letter-perfect in the lines.

Auntie Charlotte, the eldest of the kin, had some vivid memories of Andrew's babyhood. "Ye were a greedy infant," she told him. "Ye had to be fed wi' twa spoons—ye skirled sae loud the moment one of them left your mouth." Auntie Charlotte was still far behind the procession in her comprehension of Andrew's progress. She regarded his visit as highly significant. "Ye will be coming back here someday and keep a shop in the High Street," she said. Her son-in-law was a greengrocer in the High Street, a notch above shopkeepers in other streets, and to her that was the ultimate in human achievement.

Mrs. Henderson—"Ailie Fargie," the kind friend who had advanced the twenty pounds which enabled the Carnegie family to migrate to America—was still alive and she and John were doing not at all badly. That twenty-pounds outgo had set them back for a few years; but they were comfortable now, according to Dunfermline standards. For several years past they had had a nice addition to their income in the form of twenty pounds which Andrew Carnegie, out of deep gratitude for their unselfish act, had been sending Mrs. Henderson annually as "interest" on the loan. He now suggested to her, "I think I'd better pay off that loan."

"Dinna ye fash yerself about the loan, Andra," she replied. "I'm pairfectly satisfied wi' the interest."

"Oh, but I'm rich enough now to clear off the principal," he protested.

"Dinna mind the preencipal, Andra," she countered, her eyes twinkling with the humor of the situation. "It's verra weel invested as it is."

And so the "interest" payments went on.

Back home that summer of 1862 was an unhappy one for the Federal government. It did not prosper on the battlefield, and there began to be grave doubt as to the outcome of the war. Carnegie was shocked to find that sentiment in Scotland—or at least in Dunfermline—was overwhelmingly in favor of the South. Uncle George Lauder stood almost alone in upholding the rightness of the Union cause.

Due to a recurrence of his illness, Andrew spent several weeks in bed in Uncle Lauder's home. They had many talks on American affairs, and one day his uncle said to him, "Andra, it is asking a great deal, I know; but I would appreciate it if you would take my savings and invest them for me in America."

Andrew was startled by the responsibility thus thrust upon him. "How shall I invest the money, Uncle?" he asked.

"You know best, Andra," was the reply. "But if you put it into United States bonds, it will add to my pleasure; for then I can say that in the hour of her danger I have never lost faith in the Republic."

Carnegie put some of the money into government bonds, as his uncle requested; but another part of it he invested in the various enterprises with which he was connected, so that, in the end, Uncle Lauder received his money back three times over.

George, Jr., a quiet, reserved young Scot and an able mechanical engineer who had studied under Lord Kelvin, asked many questions about American business and resources, and Andrew detected in his cousin a secret longing to see and perhaps cast his lot in the new wonderland.

"With your training and ability, Dod," he said, "you could do great things over there."

Dod was noncommittal, but in time he crossed the ocean to become an important factor in the great Carnegie empire of steel.

7

‖‖

The Broken Resolution

WHILE HE WAS IN ALTOONA, CARNEGIE ENCOUNTERED IN THE
railroad shops the first iron bridge he had ever seen—a small
bridge made to carry the rails across a little creek. It had
been designed by H. J. Linville of the company's engineering staff, with the cooperation of a mechanical genius in the
shops named John L. Piper. They took out the patent
jointly. "Pipe"—as he was called by everybody in shop and
office—was the bridge builder for the railroad, though his
construction so far had all been done with wood. He was
noted for the speed with which he could replace a bridge
that had been burned—as bridges so frequently were—or
washed away. "I'd rather have Pipe at a burned bridge
than a whole engineering corps," said President Thomson.

Now Pipe was an ecstatic advocate of iron bridges.
"Wooden bridges are done for, Andy," he said again and

again. "It's nothing but iron from now on. In another twenty years there won't be a wooden bridge left on a first-class railroad. Think of having a bridge that won't burn or float away in a freshet!"

He and Aaron Schiffler, general supervisor of bridges for the railroad, left the company's employ in 1862 to form a bridge-building partnership. But they needed better business heads and more capital. Linville and Carnegie were let into the group; and the latter organized the Keystone Bridge Company, with five stockholders—Thomas N. Scott was the fifth—each of whom put in twelve hundred and fifty dollars. A bridge-building company beginning with a capital of only sixty-two hundred and fifty dollars may seem absurd to present-day minds; but costs of everything were low then, business was done on a smaller scale, and many great concerns began on what would seem to us a very slender shoestring. The stockholders had to borrow now and then, but always repaid the loans punctually. They agreed among themselves that there must be no shoddy work; every bridge was to be the best that they could produce. "An honest brig" was one of Carnegie's favorite phrases, borrowed from Thomas Carlyle.

One of the early challenges to the Keystone concern came when a railroad company which was building a westward extension of the Pennsylvania asked whether they would undertake to build a bridge across the Ohio River at Steubenville, just west of Pittsburgh, with a three-hundred-foot channel span. Steel was not yet being made in America, and even wrought iron was not produced in great quantity. To build a cast-iron railroad bridge with so long a span was a daring venture, but they accepted the risk. A high official of the railroad, when he visited the place of crossing and saw the piles of big cast-iron beams lying about, exclaimed, "I don't believe these heavy castings can be made to stand up and carry themselves, much less carry a train across the Ohio River."

But he was mistaken; that bridge stood the strains of many years, until it was removed. However, the bridge company began using wrought iron shortly after that job, first for the top chords of a truss and afterward for some other parts.

The stockholders had hoped to make a nice profit on this contract, but inflation of the currency and the rapidly rising costs of wartime were threatening to write the last line of their balance sheet in red ink when President Edgar Thomson of the Pennsylvania, aware of the situation, ordered, on his own initiative, that they be allowed an extra sum to secure them from loss—which explains in part why Carnegie, whose sense of gratitude was strong, gave his first steel plant, ten years later, Mr. Thomson's name.

In 1863, when the Civil War had brought on an income tax—a mild one compared with twentieth-century rates—

Andrew Carnegie's statement of his income for the year shows the astonishing total of $47,860.67, a remarkable figure for a man of twenty-seven. His salary as division superintendent accounted for only twenty-four hundred dollars of this total. His oil stock had brought in the largest portion; his sleeping-car, Keystone, and Adams Express stock were all contributing handsome dividends, and the remainder of his income was derived from various other investments. He was truly "a Scotchman on the make." But a portrait of him at this time exhibits the same smooth, placid face shown in his last photograph, taken eleven years before; however, his hair had darkened slightly and he had added a fringe of short, blond beard around his jaw.

One item of forty-two hundred and fifty dollars in his income memorandum is given as from "Kloman"—another business which added to the Carnegie fortune, though in this case the profits came from money he had supplied for his brother.

Andrew Kloman, an able but stubborn and quarrelsome German mechanic, had a small foundry in Allegheny and had made a reputation for his axles. With the outbreak of the war he was offered many government orders, but lacked the equipment and capital necessary to an enlarged business. Tom Miller came to the rescue and a small corporation was organized.

"I wanted to bring you into it, too, Andy," said Miller to Carnegie, "but Kloman balked at that. He's afraid of you. He thinks if you were in with us you'd be taking over the whole shebang—or trying to."

They laughed over the joke, little dreaming how soon Andy would be in the iron business after all.

The War Department orders for axles and cannon mountings poured in, and were followed by demands for other things. Still more capital was needed. One day Henry Phipps—younger brother of John, who had been accidentally killed a few years ago—said wistfully to Miller, "I'd like to get into the iron business, but I don't see how I'm going to do it."

Tom pondered a moment, pulling his mustache. . . .

He remembered how Henry—who was not yet of age— had begun his business career in his early teens by saying one day to his brother, "John, will you lend me a quarter?" As his brother looked at him inquiringly, Henry added, "It's very important."

John handed over the quarter without demur, and on the following day a brief want ad appeared in the *Dispatch:* "A willing boy wishes work." That frank, simple statement brought a prompt response from a business concern which engaged him as an errand boy, and Henry, with his parents' consent, left school and began working. He had scarcely lost a day since. . . .

Now he was bookkeeper for a powder company—"twenty years old, and I haven't gotten anywhere"; he spoke with the gloom of an old man whose life had been a failure.

Tom Miller pondered again. He had observed Henry from childhood, and knew him for a bright, conscientious young man. Moreover, he was the brother of dear old John; and that meant much.

"Have you any money to invest?" he asked.

"No," said Henry. "I've saved a little from my salary from time to time, but I've invested it all in my employers' business."

"Would you like to get into Kloman & Company?"

"I certainly would, if I had the loose cash. But"—Henry spread his hands despairingly—"I haven't it."

"I might lend you a little," said Miller. "Here's how the business stands: we're incorporated for eight thousand dollars, but it's not all paid in yet. The charter specifies that it is to be paid in from time to time, as the needs of the business demand. The company could use some more money right now for new machinery. I have a little to lend, and I could put you in for a few hundred."

"Harry" gratefully accepted the favor, and so kindly Tom Miller, instead of investing his money for himself in what was a growing and sure-fire business, advanced sixteen hundred dollars to buy shares in the company; of this amount eight hundred dollars was lent to Phipps and the other eight hundred dollars to William and Alexander Cowley, two more of those one-time Bottom Hooshiers. It would be hard to find elsewhere such a group of men, so close-knit from childhood, so loyal and true to one another.

Young Phipps went into Kloman & Company with the understanding that he was to do the bookkeeping. So, after working all day for the powder company, he gulped down a bite of dinner and hurried over to the Kloman office, to toil until late in the evening over the books. When he went into that office, it was almost inevitable that Thomas Carnegie should follow him—about the same age, they were as close to each other as were David and Jonathan. When the Kloman concern needed more cash a few months later, Andrew Carnegie supplied it for his brother, who thereupon became another partner.

But the irascible and suspicious Kloman continued to be a disturbing element. Always fearing that someone was trying to cheat him, he brought on a general row not long after this—and even committed the mad absurdity of publishing a notice in the newspapers to the effect that Thomas N. Miller was no longer a partner in his iron mill. At that, thoroughly disgusted, Miller sold out of the company.

"Well, let's start a rolling mill of our own, Tom," said Andrew Carnegie to him. "It can make iron for our bridge company, among other things."

"But we'd be competing against your brother Tom's company," objected Miller.

"There's business enough for both. They're on war contracts now; and we'd be on bridges, mostly."

So the Cyclops Iron Works was launched in 1864—and then Kloman was really furious! But he had to swallow his resentment; for the war was in its last stages, and army orders were becoming scarcer and smaller. It was not long before his partners were suggesting an amalgamation with Cyclops. Changes and developments were coming with dizzying rapidity. So, whether he liked it or not, Kloman found himself seated at the directors' table of the new combination, the Union Iron Works, along with Tom Miller and Andrew Carnegie, Miller being the largest stockholder.

"You were grievously wronged, Tom," said Andrew to him. "Now you return as a conqueror."

The two plants were not combined, but both continued roaring away at top speed.

During the last days of the war Andrew Carnegie's railroad service came to an end—much against the wishes of his superiors, Thomson and Scott. His letter of resignation was dated March 28, 1865. He also wrote a letter of appreciation and farewell to the men of the Pittsburgh Division, with whom he had become so popular that they presented him with a fine watch in farewell. His successor on the job was another of the old Allegheny boys, Bob Pitcairn.

And then, just as lightheartedly as they had done a dozen other things, Carnegie and Miller organized the Pittsburgh Locomotive Works—on a small scale, of course, turning out an engine at irregular intervals. During the preceding year Carnegie and his neighbor William Coleman had crossed over the border into Ohio to pick up some more oil land; this proved highly productive and supplied cash for more investments, including some stock in the new Union Pacific Railroad now being pushed across prairie and mountain to link the two oceans by rail for the first time. And early in 1867 the Keystone Bridge Company began work on the great, triple-arched iron bridge across the Mississippi River at St. Louis; though it was designed by Captain James B. Eads, Mr. Linville of the Keystone Company made some alterations in the plans. More than three quarters of a century later that iron bridge is still carrying an enormously increased volume of railroad and street traffic on its two levels, into and out of a vastly greater city.

A favorite book in Homewood at this time was Bayard Taylor's *Views Afoot,* describing the author's walking tour through Europe. Carnegie, an ardent traveler and sightseer, interested in history and geography, was eager to have an experience similar to Taylor's. One day he said to John Vandevort, "Vandy, if you could make three thousand dollars right now, would you spend it on a walking tour through Europe with me?"

"Would I!" retorted Vandy. "Would a duck swim or an Irishman eat potatoes?"

Oil shares were shooting up like rockets at the moment and, on Carnegie's advice, John made an investment in the "black gold" which quickly yielded the required sum. The two invited Harry Phipps, now also becoming opulent, to accompany them, and the three boarded a steamer in early spring. . . .

As the years passed, Carnegie continued to build a fortune and a great industrial empire while taking more and more frequent long vacations, which he usually spent in travel. He made it clear in his writings, his utterances, and his acts that the chief and proper aim of his life—of any man's life—was not, should not be, the manufacture of iron or steel or what not but, rather, the development of a well-rounded mind and character, and the distribution of his fortune for the good of mankind.

He worked hard and earnestly when at home, but he had no intention of working himself to death. The drudging years of his life—the long hours, six days a week and sometimes seven, for a pittance of pay—were behind him forever. Now he proposed to nourish his soul. He prided himself on having his businesses so well staffed that he could leave them at any time for months on end in perfect confidence that they would be ably and honestly conducted. The truth was that he was blessed in having so many men of ability and integrity among his kin and his boyhood friends from whom to choose his associates. And, while away, he never forgot his interests back home; never lost track of business trends, current and future. . . .

The three tourists were joined at Liverpool by John Franks, a relative of Phipps; and the quartet spent the next five months in rambling through England, France, Germany, Austria-Hungary, Switzerland, and Italy, and always in boyish high spirits. The news from home was invariably good: prices advancing, orders pouring in, mills working double shifts—the postwar boom was in full blast. Carnegie now reveled in the opportunity to stand in the spots where history, ancient and modern, was made; to hear and see all the greatest music and operas; to visit art galleries, cathedrals, castles. In Venice the palace of the Doges, the chief magistrates of the medieval Venetian republic, spurred his literary emotions deeply. In the great hall he placed his three companions in the seats once occupied by the ruling officials—Franks in the Doge's throne—and then, standing before them, he began . . .

"Most potent, grave and reverend signiors,
   My very noble and approved good masters . . ."

and so went through Othello's long speech of appeal, with grandiose gestures.

He did not fail to observe Europe's businesses, industries,

and transportation systems wherever he went, so the tour had value for him in a practical way. Nor did he forget that Union Pacific railhead pushing steadily toward the Pacific coast. From Rome he wrote to Scott, "Shouldn't the Central Transportation Co."—the Woodruff sleeper company—"be getting after a sleeping-car contract with the Union Pacific?" Scott's reply began, "You certainly do take time by the forelock, young man." George M. Pullman had obtained patents on a sleeping car so nearly like Woodruff's that one wonders why they were granted, but the ways of the Patent Office are sometimes beyond comprehension. Pullman was after the Union Pacific contract, too, but the railroad management postponed its decision for another two years.

Brother Tom was soon to marry Lucy Coleman, one of the five beautiful sisters.

"Have you decided where you're going to live?" Andrew asked after he returned from his tour.

"No," said Tom.

"How would you like to take over this house?" They were at breakfast in the dining room at Homewood.

"If Lucy likes the idea, it would suit me fine," said Tom. "But where are you going? Not still dallying with that notion of moving to New York, are you?"

"Yes, I think it advisable. You know how I've had to go there more and more often in the past few years. New York

is to the United States what London is to Great Britain—
the headquarters of all important enterprise. The bankers
there are calling on me frequently to negotiate securities,
especially with English companies, and I can get some fine
commissions in that way. Mother and I will be back here
frequently—"

"Oh, so she's going with you?" asked Tom.

"Yes," said their mother. "Andra just broke the news to
me last night, though I guessed it was coming. I dinna like
leaving Homewood; but if it's best for him, I'm willing
to go."

"And I'll keep an eye on things here," Andrew continued,
"though with such partners as you and Tom Miller and
Harry Phipps, not to mention Mr. Coleman and Pipe and
Kloman, I'm hardly needed around here any more."

Tom scoffed at that, of course; nevertheless, though still
in his middle twenties, he was already proving to be a
business genius, quite capable of handling the mills on
his own.

So he and Lucy were married—a happy marriage it
turned out to be—and took over the home, while Andrew
and his mother went to New York—to settle in a suite in the
St. Nicholas, the largest and finest hotel in the city. Margaret Carnegie took the new mode of life in her stride, as
usual; with no promise of liking it, she was resolved to be
content. As she lay down to rest that first night in her

richly appointed bedroom, her mind must have turned back to the day, almost twenty years before, when a poor immigrant Scotch weaver, his wife and two little sons, who had come to America on borrowed money, found themselves on the streets of New York, staring about them at the wonders of a great city.

Andrew Carnegie did not sit in a New York office waiting for business to come to him. He rushed immediately out to Keokuk, Iowa, to clinch a contract for bridging the Mississippi River there; and in the following year he visited the Midwest again, to sell another bridge across the big river—this one at Dubuque—largely on his argument that Keystone was now using wrought iron instead of cast iron for bridges.

At the end of 1868, sitting down to add up his year's income, he found that it came to $56,110. Then, leaning back in his chair, twiddling his pen and staring at the wall for a few moments, he decided to put on paper a resolution which had for a long time been slowly crystallizing in his mind. He leaned forward again and wrote a remarkable memorandum:

> St. Nicholas Hotel, New York,
> December, 1868.

Thirty-three and an income of $50,000 per annum!
By this time two years I can arrange all my business

so as to secure at least $50,000 per annum. Beyond this never earn—make no effort to increase fortune, but spend the surplus each year for benevolent purposes. Cast aside business forever, except for others.

Settle in Oxford and get a thorough education, making the acquaintance of literary men—this will take three years' active work—pay especial attention to speaking in public. Settle then in London and purchase a controlling interest in some newspaper or live review, and give the general management of it attention, taking a part in public matters, especially those connected with education and improvement of the poorer classes.

Man must have an idol—the amassing of wealth is one of the worst species of idolatry—no idol more debasing than the worship of money. Whatever I engage in I must push inordinately; therefore should I be careful to choose that life which will be the most elevating in its character. To continue much longer overwhelmed by business cares and with most of my thoughts wholly upon the way to make more money in the shortest time, must degrade me beyond hope of permanent recovery. I will resign business at thirty-five, but during the ensuing two years I wish to spend the afternoons in receiving instruction and reading systematically.

Little did he dream how difficult it would be to escape the snares of business within two years, or ever. Not two years, but twenty years were to pass before his retirement. However, this statement of preference for culture over money-making proves the sincerity of his preaching in later years that wealth is not rightfully the property of the millionaire, but should be regarded as only held in trust by him for the public benefit. Cynics sneered at this philosophy as hypocritical, but Carnegie meant it; and the time came when he began to make his words good, though he never gave away all his fortune.

He never went to Oxford for study, but he labored constantly to improve himself in public speaking and to increase his knowledge of history, philosophy, literature, and the arts. His visits to England and elsewhere abroad, combining business and self-culture, became more frequent. He was pulled in two directions: the lure of business success was irresistible, though his real, deeper love was for the higher things. He toiled away wholeheartedly during the two years he had allotted himself before retirement. He went to John W. Garrett, the great magnate of the Baltimore & Ohio Railroad, and sold him contracts for two bridges, crossing the Ohio River at Wheeling and at Parkersburg. He met George M. Pullman, who was beginning to manufacture his sleeping cars in Chicago, and with his unerring instinct for judging character he saw the stuff of business greatness in Pullman.

"We must sue that fellow for infringement," said his associates hotly.

"I don't think so," retorted Carnegie. "You know how lawsuits drag along for years through the courts, and the lawyers get all the money. Pullman's location at Chicago gives him a better chance at the Middle Western and far Western railroads than we have and, furthermore, that young man is destined to do big things in industry. We'd better join hands with him if we can."

Fate seemed to be smiling when Carnegie found himself, one summer evening in '69, walking up the front steps of the St. Nicholas almost alongside of George Pullman. The Union Pacific directors were to meet in New York on the following day and would then award the sleeping-car contract.

"Good evening, Mr. Pullman," said Carnegie cheerily.

Pullman merely grunted a sour "Good evening," but Carnegie was not disconcerted.

"How odd that we should meet here!" was his next remark, which didn't even win a reply. Baffled for only a moment, Carnegie exclaimed with a boyish laugh, "Here we are together! Don't you think we are making a pair of nice fools of ourselves?"

The rival manufacturer stopped and glared at his challenger. "What do you mean?" he demanded.

"This Union Pacific business. What's the good of our

fighting each other about it—destroying the very advantages we hope to obtain?"

That won a hearing. "What do you propose to do about it?" asked Pullman.

"Unite!" exclaimed Carnegie. "Make a joint proposition to the Union Pacific, your party and mine, and organize a company."

"What would you call it?"

Carnegie knew that that was the crucial question, and he had his answer ready: "The Pullman Palace Car Company."

Pullman's icy countenance thawed at once. "Come into my room and talk it over," he invited.

And so the deal was made. Good-natured Theodore Woodruff, though a little unhappy over the naming of the new company, agreed to the plan when he was shown what financial advantages were likely to result from the consolidation.

But steel was the thing which finally caught Carnegie firmly in its toils. Steel had been made on a small scale since ancient times; but its manufacture was slow and difficult—really an art—until Henry Bessemer, over in England, devised a process by which it could be cast in large pieces, such as rails and bridge beams. Now Andrew Carnegie's future career was definitely patterned for him.

8

The Age of Steel

UNTIL THE CIVIL WAR, AMERICAN RAILWAY TRAINS HAD ALL run on iron rails. The first steel rails were imported from England in 1863. But after the war American iron manufacturers began to turn to the Bessemer process. Carnegie was not greatly interested until he saw steel being made in England during one of his bond-selling visits over there. He became excited at once. He rushed from the pier at New York to Pittsburgh and cried to his partners, "The day of iron is past! Steel! Steel is king! We must begin making steel rails—begin at once!"

He had expected the stodgy Kloman to oppose the idea; but he was not prepared to find his other partners, even his brother Tom, against him, too. However, they were iron men; they could not change their habits and their thinking so suddenly. They had just built a new blast furnace, the largest in America (christened The Lucy, in honor of Tom's

94

wife), and that had cost a pot of money. Finally they—
especially Tom—were quieter, more conservative; they
couldn't avoid a feeling that Andrew was a bit wild and
impetuous. Some men of his time always believed that his
success was due as much to luck as to genius and hard work.
Tow knew better, though he was not always ready to go
along with his brother's new ideas.

"Go easy, Andy," he advised, leaning back comfortably
in his chair. "There's great excitement over steel right now,
and it'll be overdone. Iron! Iron is the real foundation of
all American industry, and it will continue to be. We are
doing well, making money in iron. Why sink a lot of money
in something out of our line?"

The other partners agreed with Tom, and after some
futile argument Andrew said, "Well, if you boys won't come
in with me, I'll have to start a separate corporation, with
an entirely new group of partners."

"Oh, I'm not saying I won't invest some money in your
scheme, Andy," said Tom. "Maybe the other fellows will,
too, in a small way. But I don't think our present firm ought
to attempt it."

"Perhaps you're right," agreed Andrew.

So he brought together a group which included the
Homewood neighbors Coleman and Stewart; the railroad
executives Thomson and Scott; and—chief partner of all—
David McCandless, a wholesale dry-goods merchant. Once

in the old Rebecca Street days, when the Carnegie family was at the lowest ebb of its fortunes, Mr. McCandless had delicately offered, through Aunt Aitken, to make them a loan. The offer was declined, but Andrew never forgot the kindness.

His partners in the iron works all bought stock in modest quantities; and Brother Tom recommended the site for the mill, twelve miles up the Monongahela from Pittsburgh, at the village of Braddock, on the very spot where the British General Braddock had been so disastrously defeated and slain by a French and Indian force in 1755. At this site the steel mill would have access to two major railroads and, through the Monongahela, to the Ohio River.

"I am going to call it the Edgar Thomson Steel Works, in honor of my dear old friend of railroad days," said Carnegie.

But Mr. Thomson, though a large stockholder, was rather cool to the idea. "I'm not so sure I want my name connected with American steel rails, Andy," he said. "Those made so far would do no credit to anybody. Better call it something else."

"But we're going to make good rails, Mr. Thomson," protested Carnegie. "It's possible now to manufacture steel in this country as good as is made anywhere in the world. I intend to see that we get the same reputation for our rails that Keystone bridges and Kloman axles enjoy."

And at length Thomson consented.

The building of the mill had not progressed very far when the financial panic of 1873 burst upon the land. "Aha!" said many critics. "That brash Andy Carnegie's luck has turned against him at last. He will be ruined!" He had $250,000 of his own money in the project, mostly earned as commissions on bond sales. As luck would have it, he had chosen that year to begin his benefactions by giving a public bathhouse to his native Dunfermline. He sold his Pullman stock and various other securities to raise cash, and the building of the mill was delayed but a short time. Thenceforth he disposed of his interests in other businesses, one after another, to concentrate on steel and iron. "I determined that the wise policy was to put all my good eggs into one basket," he said, "and then watch that basket."

But he had already become entangled in a railroad investment which gave him some trouble. At the insistence of his old friend Scott he had invested $250,000 in the stock of the Texas & Pacific Railroad, which Scott was promoting, and now that company was bankrupt. A large loan fell due; and when Junius S. Morgan, the Yankee-born banker in London with whom Andrew had had several transactions, said that if Carnegie would endorse the note he would renew it, Carnegie refused to do so.

"Would you bring your old friends to ruin, Andy, by refusing to stand by them?" Scott reproached him.

"Well, if it is a question of the ruin of your group or the ruin of my business, my partners and their families," retorted Carnegie, "I'll have to decide in their favor. I tried to persuade you not to start building the road on too little capital, Mr. Scott; not to launch a thousand miles of track on temporary loans—you know that. But you wouldn't listen to me. Then, when I came back from Europe, you told me you had a quarter million in stock reserved for me, and for old times' sake I accepted it. I still believe the T. & P. will eventually be a money-maker, but I can't endorse that paper. It would mean risking my investments in the mills and the safety of my partners, and I must not do that."

It was a hard decision to make, though he made it without hesitation. It gave him more pain than any other financial trial he had had to endure, for Scott's friendship was never the same thereafter. But Carnegie was justified when the panic struck. It was known that he was involved with Scott in Texas & Pacific; and the Exchange Bank of Pittsburgh, the financial house for the Carnegie companies, was greatly alarmed, supposing that Carnegie had endorsed much Texas & Pacific paper and would therefore be drawn down in its crash, which would endanger his companies at Pittsburgh. As the Exchange Bank held notes of the Carnegie companies for considerable sums, the directors summoned him to appear before them at once; and he hurried from New York to answer the call.

Appearing before the grim-faced board, he said calmly, "It's true that I own two hundred and fifty thousand dollars' worth of Texas & Pacific stock; but it's all paid for with my own cash, and I haven't endorsed any notes for them."

They found that hard to believe.

"My name isn't on one dollar's worth of their paper," he insisted. "That would be speculation, and I regard speculation as the greatest curse of the business world. A stock exchange is little or no better than a gambling house," he went on, and that continued to be his firm opinion throughout his life. "The only loans on which I am jointly responsible are those given by you to our local companies for increasing our equipment; and I am willing to put every dollar and every bit of property I have back of them, to show you that they are enough to cover the loans—"

"Oh, we are not in the least worried about those loans, Carnegie," broke in the bank president. "It's just this Texas & Pacific matter—we heard you were endorsing their paper—"

"You'll never find me engaged in speculation," said Carnegie, "You'll never find me in Wall Street. And, as for endorsing, I make it a practice never to sign a note unless I think I can see my way clear to paying it at maturity, and unless I have assets which will cover it if I can't pay it then. As a Western friend of mine says, I never go in deeper than I can wade."

Carnegie emerged from that conference with the profound respect of the business and financial world. Far from being a rash adventurer, he was almost the only big industrialist who came through the panic unscathed. He even took over the shares of some of those in his steel company who were caught short and needed money; and while the iron and steel industry in general was almost at a standstill, the Edgar Thomson mill continued to rise at Braddock all through the depression. Carnegie was putting into practice another important fact which he had grasped—that the time to build, if you have the money, is during a depression, when materials are cheap; then you are ready to begin operations with an advantage when prosperity returns. Those who wait for better times must pay higher prices for building materials; hence they have a costlier plant and make smaller profits.

Carnegie's acumen accounted for the fact that, when it began operations in 1875, the Edgar Thomson mill could undersell other manufacturers of rails, and consequently had large orders when some other plants were idle. Its success was further assured when Carnegie procured the services of the best steelmaker in America—Captain "Bill" Jones, Welsh-born and a Civil War veteran, who had left a rival concern in disgust because his ability was unrecognized. Here is seen another of the secrets of Carnegie's success—his rare judgment of men. An eminent manufacturer once said of him, "He exceeded anyone I ever knew in his ability

to pick a man from one place and put him in another with
the maximum effect." He said he had known Carnegie to
take a man whom others considered to be of little or no
account, put him in an important position, "and he would
fit just like the tumblers in a Yale lock. As a picker of men
for certain positions, I do not think he has ever had his
equal."

"I have no shadow of claim," Carnegie said frankly, "to
rank as inventor, chemist, investigator, or mechanism." He
just knew how to find the right men and to get the best
service from them—not "head service or hand service," he
pointed out; "it is heart service that counts. You must cap-
ture and keep the heart of the original and able man before
his brain can do its best."

He already had the heart loyalty of Cousin Dod, another
indispensable man whom he added to the organization in
the 1870s. His steel company had acquired coal mines for
its own use, just as the iron and bridge companies had done.
Mr. Coleman had long worried over the dross, the waste,
from their coal mines; and once when he was in England,
George Lauder showed him a process which he had devised for washing and coking this waste. Coleman came
home enthusiastic. "Now you must come over here, Dod,"
wrote Naig, "and show us this process of yours." He came
and set up the first coal-washing plants in America, bringing about an enormous saving to the companies. "We
mustn't let this man go back to England," said the partners

to one another. And so Lauder stayed, became a partner in the Carnegie enterprises, and died wealthy.

Dunfermline supplied a remarkable number of recruits to the army of steel. Walking through the works one day, Carnegie was accosted by the superintendent, who said, "Mr. Carnegie, do you know you have a relative working here?"

"No," was the surprised reply.

"You have; and he's a darned good mechanic, too. I didn't know he was kin to you until recently."

"May I speak to him?"

"Certainly." The superintendent led the way to a young man working at a machine. "Here he is," he said. "Tom, this is Mr. Carnegie."

"What is your name?" asked the magnate.

"Thomas Morrison—son of Robert," was the reply.

"What! My cousin Bob?"

"Yes."

"How did you happen to come here?"

"I thought we could better ourselves."

"We?" repeated Carnegie. "Whom have you with you?"

"My wife."

The boss studied him curiously. "Why didn't you come to me, your relative, first?" he asked. "I could have given you an introduction; might have given you a better start."

"I didn't feel I needed help, if only I got a chance," retorted Morrison, looking straight into the older man's eyes.

"There spoke the true Morrison!" exclaimed Carnegie in describing the episode. "Taught to depend on himself, and independent as Lucifer."

Without any "influence" from his powerful cousin Thomas rose in a few years to the superintendency of a new plant at Duquesne, became a partner, and eventually he, too, was a millionaire.

Carnegie bought a cottage on the very summit of the Alleghenies, near Cresson, Pennsylvania, in a region remindful of the Highlands of Scotland; and there, at the first sign of spring, he and his mother would hie themselves. After a month or so, with several flying visits to New York or Pittsburgh, he would leave for his vacation in Scotland or on the Continent. For several years his mother accompanied him abroad, though as she neared seventy she sometimes remained at the Allegheny cottage. At the end of summer the returning traveler, or the two of them, would hasten to Cresson again, to remain until the leaves had fallen.

Sometimes when Carnegie drove into Cresson, a strapping, bright-faced youth in his middle teens would offer to hold his horse while he went into a store. As the steel magnate drove off, the boy would accept his dime or quarter tip and stride away whistling. This boy at fifteen drove the stage which ran between Cresson and his home town of Loretto, a few miles away. Carnegie did not know his name then, but the time came when he knew it well.

9

A Memorable Year

THE YEAR 1881 WAS FILLED WITH NOTABLE EVENTS IN ANDREW Carnegie's life. Early in that year the promise he had made his brother in boyhood was fulfilled when Carnegie Brothers & Company was incorporated with a capital of five million dollars, of which Andrew owned a little more than half. This was not an ordinary corporation; its owners were not stockholders—they were "associates." The stock was not to be sold to anyone outside the group unless Andrew Carnegie decided to take a new and promising young partner—which meant that none of the stock was ever to appear in that mart so abhorrent to Carnegie, the Stock Exchange.

Into this new corporation were merged the Edgar Thomson Steel Works, the Union Iron Mills, the Lucy Furnaces —there were several of them now—coal mines, and coke ovens. Carnegie steel not only had laid thousands of miles of the main railroads of the country but had gone into the New York elevated railroads and many bridges—including the Brooklyn Bridge, the first great span across the East River at New York and, for the time being, the wonder of the age.

And that was the year when Carnegie made his first gift of a public-library building—quite appropriately to Dunfermline. No other city in the world would have appreciated such a gift more, or as much.

When he was consulting the architect about plans for the building, the latter said, "I should like to have a picture of your coat of arms, Mr. Carnegie. It ought to be in the building somewhere." Americans who acquire wealth but have no ancestral armorial bearings frequently employ a heraldic expert to fake a coat of arms for them, and the architect presumed that Carnegie had followed this practice. But not so.

"Bless you, man, I haven't any coat of arms," retorted the persistent democrat. "If you must have a design of some sort," he suggested later, "why don't you just carve over the door a rising sun beaming its rays everywhere, and the words 'Let there be light'?" And so it was done.

Carnegie planned a coaching trip through England and Scotland from south to north, to terminate at Dunfermline for the laying of the library cornerstone. There were eleven

105

in the merry party who crossed the ocean together, including his mother and himself. The others were associates and friends—some accompanied by their wives—who could get away from their desks. On the journey northward seventy-year-old Margaret Carnegie, sitting high up beside the driver of the four-horse team, was perhaps the liveliest of the party. More than once, when they crossed a brook, she took off her shoes and stockings and waded in the water. Once she kilted her skirts and danced a Highland fling on a bit of greensward. Evidently she knew that this was to be her last trip to Scotland, and she was making the most of it.

As the party ferried across the Firth of Forth—where they were joined by Uncle Lauder—they learned that the whole countryside was thronging to Dunfermline. As they approached the old city, the crowds increased. They saw the banners of Scotland, England, and the United States flying side by side from the old royal palace. At the outskirts a triumphal arch had been erected, and here the Provost, the Town Council and magistrates, all in their robes of office, awaited them. An address of welcome was spoken, not by one of the officials but, very appropriately, by a weaver—and it was well done, too. Then a mile-long procession—bands and bagpipers, lodges and workmen's guilds, including thousands of women and girls from the linen mills, carrying British and American flags—wound through the gaily decorated streets of the growing city, passing under banners and arches inscribed "Welcome, Carnegie." Twice they paused—at the stone cottage where Andrew was born, and at that other little house where his mother had kept her "sweetie shop." In the hush which prevailed at this second stop, the mellow sound of the Abbey bell brought a gush of tears to the Steel King's eyes.

Luncheon followed . . . a tour of old haunts and landmarks . . . and then the cornerstone ceremony, where the principal address was delivered by the Earl of Rosebery. The trustees had expected that Carnegie himself would undertake the symbolic formality of laying the stone; but he requested that the honor be given to his mother, for whom his admiration seemed to increase year by year. He sometimes touched her forehead with his finger and said, "Here is where Tom and I get our brains." As he had expected, his mother—a distinguished figure in black silk with a crown of white hair—went through the rite with perfect self-possession and grace; after spreading the mortar with a silver trowel, she gave the rock three taps with the handle and announced in a clear voice that carried all over the vast assemblage, "I pronounce this memorial stone duly and properly laid, and may God bless the undertaking."

Her son, who always fancied himself as an author, recounted this coaching tour in a book entitled *An American Four-in-Hand in Britain,* which was published in 1882.

That year 1881 saw the appearance of a competitor—a new steel plant being built by Pittsburgh promoters at Homestead, a little way down the Monongahela from the Edgar Thomson Works and on the opposite bank of the stream. But the new plant was cursed by labor troubles and by a slight business recession which cut down the volume of orders. Then the directors began quarreling among themselves, and finally agreed that they were ready to quit. An emissary approached Carnegie—who had been watching the course of events and expecting this outcome—and asked him if he would care to take over Homestead. He admitted that he would. A delegation next visited his office with their hearts in their mouths, expecting to be squeezed in traditional Scotch fashion.

"What are your terms?" they asked.

"We will replace every dollar you have invested in your plant," he replied, "pay each of you for your stock—in stock of the Carnegie corporation or, if you prefer it, in cash."

It was several seconds before they could recover their breath. Then they began speaking up emphatically in favor of getting cash for their shares. They didn't ask for a moment's time to consider; they had had enough of the steel business—all but one of them, that is; he was a Mr. Singer, who asked for twenty-four hours to think it over. On the following morning he reappeared and asked, "Did you really mean what you said yesterday? Would you take me in as a partner?"

"Of course I would," replied the smiling Carnegie, offering his hand. "Shake, partner!"

Mr. Singer never regretted his decision, though his former partners suffered unending remorse for their shortsightedness. Steel was just then coming into its own. To rails were added locomotives and cars, bridges, machinery, boilers, pipe, cable, barbed wire, and—to cap them all—the framing of that awe-inspiring newcomer, the skyscraper.

There was another who came into the picture in 1881—a young man from western Pennsylvania named Henry Clay Frick, who had gone in very shrewdly for coke-making. By '81 he controlled eighty per cent of the coke business in the Connellsville region, which produces the finest coking coal in the world; but he had also gone heavily into debt. Nevertheless he chose that year to marry a Pittsburgh girl. For some time Carnegie had had an eye on him, with a view to annexing him as a partner. He was too able a man to leave outside the organization. The two met and closed a deal; and when Frick and his bride came to New York on their honeymoon, Carnegie invited them to dinner. His mother was the only other guest, and at the end of the meal the host rose and proposed a toast—the health of his good friends Mr. and Mrs. Frick—and added, "Mr. Frick and I are about to become partners."

This was for the benefit of his mother, the only one not yet in on the secret.

"A verra good thing for Mr. Freeck, Andra," she promptly rejoined. "But what do we get out of it?"

Shortly afterward, on January 1, 1882, the H. C. Frick Coke Company was organized, with more than ten per cent of the stock owned by the Carnegie group. This, however, increased until they had a dominant interest, though Frick continued to dictate the policy of the company—meanwhile increasing his holdings in Carnegie steel.

Captain Bill Jones—now such a noted figure in the world of steel that he was once called upon to go over to London and read a paper before the British Iron and Steel Institute —took over at Homestead. Carnegie had tried to make Jones a partner in his favorite way—by setting aside a block of stock for him, to be paid for out of dividends. But Jones objected, arguing that to become one of the company would injure his standing with the workmen.

"They would think I was putting on airs," he said.

"What do you suggest?" asked Carnegie. "What you're doing for us must be recognized in some way."

"Well, you might give me a whale of a big salary," replied Jones.

"We'll do it!" The boss slapped the desk. "From now on, you draw the same salary as the President of the United States"—which was then fifty thousand dollars a year.

"That's the talk, Andy!" was Captain Bill's acceptance.

Carnegie was a boss who was always prodding—though good-naturedly—and asking for frequent reports of progress and conditions. When notified that "we broke all records for making steel last week," he would reply, "Congratulations! Why not do it every week?"—or he might ask for the cost sheets. When he was told that "Number 8 furnace broke all records today," he asked what the other ten furnaces were doing. Bill Jones sometimes squirmed under this needling, and he hated making out detailed reports and cost sheets. He was a great steelmaker, but statistics bored him. Carnegie once said to him, speaking of his summer trips abroad, "No matter how tired I am, when once I am on the steamer, a half-hour out, with the New Jersey highlands sinking on the horizon behind me, all my cares and weariness slip from me; you've no idea what a relief it is, Bill."

"And you've no idea what a relief it is to the rest of us, Andy," retorted blunt Captain Jones.

One day when he was supposed to bring one of his reports to the boss's office, there appeared instead a beaming, round-faced young six-footer who said he had been sent by the Captain. He handed the concise, tabulated report to Carnegie, who studied it for a few minutes in silence before looking up.

111

"The Captain says you know all about the works," Carnegie remarked.

"Well, sir, I do know a lot about them," replied the young man, and that sunny smile broke forth as usual.

"And your name is—" The magnate glanced down at the Captain's note.

"Charles M. Schwab."

"Well, Charlie," said the chief, "now tell me just how we are getting on." He leaned back in his chair for an elaboration of the report, and he got it with a fullness that astonished him. This young fellow did indeed seem to know all about the works. Carnegie fired scores of questions at him and he answered them all, promptly and fully. Meanwhile there seemed to be something familiar about the young man's face.

"Have we ever met before, Charlie?" was the next question.

"Yes, sir. I used to hold your horse for you sometimes at Cresson."

A new partner was in the making, then and there.

Drawn by the lure of steel, young Schwab at eighteen had gone down to Braddock and found a job in a grocery store, where he sold Captain Jones his regular supply of cigars. One day the youth said, "Captain Jones, can't you give me a job in the mill?"

Jones had already taken a great liking to the young fellow. "Why, yes, Charlie, I think I can," he replied.

It was just as simple as that. And the better he knew Charlie, the more he liked and admired him. Schwab was brilliant in intellect, tireless in energy and devotion to his work, and one of the most winsome personalities that ever lived. He began at once to study books on the chemistry of steelmaking, and very soon, as Captain Bill had said, he knew all about the works. He was just the type to endear himself to Andrew Carnegie. From the moment of that first interview he became one of the Steel King's "boys," and eventually the closest to him of them all. Within six months from the day Jones gave him his first job, Schwab was assistant manager at Braddock; and he won the place strictly on merit. Five years later, when Captain Jones was killed in a disastrous accident at the plant, Charlie was superintendent of the Homestead mill, which under him was making a remarkable record for production.

"Mr. Schwab," Carnegie told a Congressional committee several years later, "is a genius. I have never met his equal."

Schwab was taken into partnership in the same way as were several other young men during the years that followed. A block of the Carnegie-corporation stock was sold to him at par—there's no telling what it would have brought if it had ever appeared on the Stock Exchange—and was soon paid for out of dividends; thereafter he was on velvet.

113

All the young partners thus chosen became wealthy. Carnegie used to say that the Gloucester fishing fleet was to his mind the ideal business organization, in that none of the hands received wages; they all just shared in the profits.

Carnegie was a keen judge of men, and he had great confidence in one who he had decided was a good man; in Charlie Schwab his confidence was almost complete. Once when Schwab was in command at Braddock, he urged his chief to let him build a new converting mill. "With it we'll save fifty cents a ton on steel," he promised.

It was a time when money was not too plentiful in the corporation's treasury, but Carnegie finally said, "All right, go ahead."

The mill was built, and one day the boss went out there to look it over. He expected that Schwab would be his usual effervescent self, bouncing with pride and promise of great work to be done. But as they went along, Carnegie's keen mind detected a lack of enthusiasm; Charlie was just like a professional guide, explaining the thing in a routine manner.

Finally his chief said, "Charlie, there's something wrong here. I can see that you are disappointed. There's something wrong with this mill, isn't there?"

"No, Mr. Carnegie," was the reply. "It is just exactly what I told you it would be, and we have reduced our costs as I said we would. But if I had it to do all over again, there is one thing which has just recently been discovered that I would introduce here; by it I am sure we could save a dollar instead of fifty cents a ton."

"Well, what does that mean?" asked Carnegie. "Can you change this mill?"

"No, it would mean tearing this down and rebuilding it."

"Why, then," exclaimed Carnegie without a moment's hesitation, "that's the right thing to do! It would be foolish not to profit by anything that may have been overlooked or discovered after the work was done. Tear it down and do it over again."

He had not even asked what the discovery was, though of course Schwab told him immediately, And afterward Charlie remembered gratefully that he didn't say, "Why didn't you think of this before?" No wonder Schwab inscribed on the photograph of himself which he gave to his chief in later years, "To my Dearest Friend and 'Master.'"

And yet Carnegie would sometimes scold his "boy" good-naturedly for "extravagance." "Charlie, I don't understand you," he would say. "Here you are, a poor boy, born in the country, and yet you don't understand the value of money. You spend and spend for new work extensions all the time as if we had money unlimited." But Charlie would argue back at him, and it was noticeable that the chief never forbade any of his favorite protégé's projects.

In later years Schwab enjoyed telling of one forenoon—

after he himself had moved to New York, but in preautomobile days—when he went up to Carnegie's home to consult him on a business matter. In characteristic Schwab fashion he called, not a hansom cab or a one-horse hack, but a carriage, and told the driver to wait while he went in to talk to the boss. The conference lasted longer than he expected, and Mr. Carnegie finally invited him to stay for lunch. Forgetting all about the carriage, Charlie accepted the invitation—and prolonged the talk after lunch. Finally the butler appeared in the doorway.

"Beg pardon, Mr. Schwab," he said, "but do you want the carriage to wait any longer?"

Charlie's face was beet-red and he sputtered confusedly as he tried to regain his composure. His old boss didn't say a word—just sat and looked at him with a whimsically humorous expression. Words weren't necessary.

10

Marriage and the Gospel of Wealth

A LOVER OF HORSEBACK RIDING, CARNEGIE RODE IN CENTRAL
Park with various young ladies—one of whom, Miss Louise
Whitfield, daughter of a New York wholesale merchant, he
liked particularly well. After a year or two of her compan-
ionship he realized that he was in love, for the first time
in his life. It was a quiet courtship; Miss Whitfield finally
accepted his proposal, and for some time they were engaged.

Meanwhile, during his annual visits abroad, he was estab-
lishing many friendships and ties in Great Britain. Among
his close friends were Matthew Arnold and Herbert Spencer, the philosopher; Viscount Morley, the Earl of Elgin,
Sir William Vernon Harcourt, and Lord Bryce; several
prime ministers—including Gladstone, Rosebery, Balfour,
and Campbell-Bannerman—and, of course, all the leading

117

industrialists and bankers. He served a term as President of the British Iron and Steel Institute. He wrote frequently for British magazines, airing his views on many subjects. Even the publication, in 1886, of his book *Triumphant Democracy,* in which he extolled America's pre-eminence over the Old World, did not decrease his popularity in Britain. In conversations with prominent British friends he actually advocated the abolition of the monarchy and the establishment of a republic. He bought several newspapers in the United Kingdom to promote his radical views; but they made no impression on the British, who were too conservative for him. And yet he was their most popular American. One after another, English, Scotch, and Irish communities gave him the "freedom of the city" with an elaborate scroll and appropriate ceremonies. All told, he received fifty-nine of these honors—more than any other person. Mr. Gladstone, who stood second, had only seventeen! There was even talk in England of electing the American magnate to Parliament.

Miss Whitfield became increasingly appalled by all this, and especially by the thought of his sitting in Parliament. At last, arguing that she could be of little help to him in this greatly expanded life, she gently broke the engagement.

In 1886 Carnegie contracted typhoid fever on the hilltop at Cresson, and during his illness sorrow smote him heavily.

Both his mother and his brother became ill and died. Old age had much to do with Mrs. Carnegie's death, but Tom's passing, at the age of forty-three, was an unexpected disaster. When the news was broken to Andrew, he was too disheartened to care whether he lived or died. He had lost the two who were dearest in all the world to him . . . two valued counselors and aides. Tom, who was chairman of all the Carnegie enterprises, had been as a right arm to him; he did not see how he could get along without him.

For some time he lay in deep depression. Gradually he regained a little strength of body and spirit, and then he could not banish the ever-recurring thought of another "dearest person"—Louise Whitfield. Perhaps she would relent now. As soon as he could sit up he wrote her a letter, begging her to consent to a renewal of their engagement. When he was able to travel, Dr. F. S. Denny, an eminent New York physician who had been called to Cresson to attend him, took him to the Denny home in New York, where, under the care of the doctor and his wife, he convalesced. Here Miss Whitfield called on him to say that his bereavement had caused her to reconsider, and that her answer now was Yes. After all she loved him—and "I feel that you really need me now," she told him. "I think I can be a real helpmeet to you."

They were married on April 22, 1887, and spent their honeymoon on the Isle of Wight. There Uncle Lauder and a Morrison cousin came down for a short visit. Uncle Lauder procured for them a summer's lease on Kilgraston Castle, the ancestral home of the Grants, in the Grampian Hills of Scotland. On their way northward they stopped at Edinburgh, where Carnegie laid the cornerstone of the library he was giving to the old capital. At ceremonies granting him the "freedom of the city," Lord Rosebery delivered the principal address. From Edinburgh they went to Dunfermline, where the bride was delighted with the town and the kinspeople, and they with her. More than one said to her husband, "I'm surprised that she married ye, Andra"— to which he would retort, "You're no more surprised than I am."

No marriage was ever happier. Mrs. Carnegie, her husband said, became even more Scotch than he was. The old cities and towns, the hills and lochs, the flowers, all delighted her. She was particularly fond of bagpipe music and suggested that it would be pleasant to have a bagpiper greet them every morning upon arising, and pipe them in to dinner. The wish was quickly fulfilled. Cluny Macpherson, the head of his clan, sent a piper to them with a high recommendation, and he preceded them as they entered Kilgraston Castle.

That was a jolly summer. Most of the time there was a swarm of guests—British and American—in the castle, including as many of the Dunfermline kin as could come. When the Carnegies returned to New York in the fall they took the piper with them, though they must have found it a little difficult to fit him into the fairly large but unpretentious house at Fifty-first Street and Fifth Avenue. He was in his own realm during the following summer, however, when the Carnegies leased Cluny Castle from The Macpherson for the season—as they continued to do for ten summers.

Carnegie had for several years been giving away large sums of money. He had remarked to Gladstone in 1887 that it was a disgrace for a man to die rich—a statement which he found it hard to live up to in the end. In 1889 he wrote two articles for the *North American Review* on what came to be called his "gospel of wealth." He said there are three ways of disposing of wealth: it can be bequeathed to the rich man's relatives; it can be left for public benefactions after his death; or it can be given away during his lifetime. Carnegie preferred the last plan. When money is left as a public legacy, sometimes the real object or wish of the donor is not attained. And anyhow, he said, "This is only a means of disposing of wealth, provided a man is content to wait until he is dead before he becomes of much use to the world." He thought legacies should be more heavily taxed, to discourage this practice. "It is impossible," he said, "to extol any man greatly for leaving what he cannot take with him. . . . Nothing counts for much that is left by a man at his death. Such funds are torn from him, not given by him."

As far back as 1881 he had written to the Mayor of Pittsburgh offering $250,000 for a public library, provided the city would agree to appropriate $15,000 a year to maintain it. Strange as it may seem, some prominent citizens were opposed to the plan. The *Pittsburgh Times,* in an editorial, said that books, magazines, and newspapers were so inexpensive that a library was not as necessary as a public park, and suggested that Mr. Carnegie give a park to the city. It was also pointed out that the city had no power to raise money by taxation for such a purpose. And so the matter drifted along for six years before the legislature passed an enabling act for maintenance of the library. In the meantime Allegheny, which was not yet annexed to Pittsburgh, had asked for and received a Carnegie library, together with the memorial to Colonel Anderson already mentioned. President Benjamin Harrison journeyed from Washington to make the address at the dedication.

When Pittsburgh was finally ready in '87 to receive the gift, the philanthropist realized the city had grown so greatly in the past few years that it would need more library facilities for research and circulation than he had foreseen, also an art gallery and an auditorium. So he offered a million now, provided the city would promise $40,000 a year for maintenance. He soon added another $100,000 and then a million for the art gallery; and so the Carnegie Institute grew and grew and grew, until within a quarter-century its benefactor had put $28,000,000 into it.

His gifts kept increasing in number and size. For years he had been giving money—in sums of $10,000 to $100,000 or more—to colleges in need of new buildings or facilities, including libraries. In several instances he gave money to enlarge and improve a city's existing library. In Atlanta, for example, the Young Men's Library Association had been struggling for thirty years to maintain a public library, with but poor success. Carnegie offered $125,000 to enlarge the library and put it on a better footing. Several years passed before the task could be finally accomplished; but when the building was at last reopened, a marble bust of Carnegie—paid for with pennies contributed by the children of Atlanta—was placed just inside the entrance as a memorial to the generous donor. He gave $1,500,000 to the engineering societies of New York City for the erection of a fifteen-story clubhouse in central Manhattan, with separate quarters for each society, a fine library, and an auditorium.

Always an ardent lover of music, he had begun giving pipe organs to struggling churches. But few of his gifts have given more joy to millions than has the great concert auditorium at Fifty-seventh Street and Seventh Avenue in New York which for several decades has been echoing to the strains of all the greatest in the realm of music. Though the donor called it the New York Music Hall, its trustees soon rechristened it Carnegie Hall—the name by which it has long been known and loved. The noted Russian composer Peter Tchaikovsky was brought over in 1891 to conduct the

123

opening concert, which included one of his own great symphonies. He was invited to the Carnegie home for dinner, and during the evening his host gave an imitation of him conducting an orchestra—did it, Tchaikovsky wrote afterward, "so solemnly, so well and so like me that I myself was delighted."

Steel and munitions makers have been accused of promoting wars for their own profit. Whether this is true or not, Andrew Carnegie was never one of the warmakers; indeed, from the time he began to think about world affairs he longed for peace among all nations. An episode of this period proves the sincerity of his attitude.

President Harrison and his Secretary of State, James G. Blaine, were both good friends of Carnegie and, as he had become known as an advocate of world understanding, he was appointed one of the delegates to the Pan-American Congress which assembled in Washington in October, 1889.

By way of hospitality the United States government treated the Latin Americans to a six-thousand-mile tour of forty-one cities, from Boston to St. Louis, showing them Niagara Falls and other scenic wonders; a burning natural-gas well in Ohio; and some of the steel mills and furnaces around Pittsburgh, with Carnegie himself as escort. All this the visitors regarded as ostentation. And they were irritated by the military review staged for their entertainment in Washington; they considered that we were flaunting our military prowess in order to force them to follow our leadership. Add to this the fact that they had a number of minor quarrels among themselves, and it is not hard to see why the conference failed to accomplish its purpose of bringing about better understanding among the Americas.

Two years later the Republic of Chile was almost in a state of revolution, and the United States, an innocent bystander, was in bad odor with both factions. United States citizens were unsafe on Chilean streets; yet some sailors from an American vessel went ashore in Valparaiso, were attacked by a mob, and two of them were killed and eighteen injured. The United States demanded an explanation, Chile replied curtly, and in Washington there was talk of war.

Carnegie, much disturbed, decided to go down to Washington and see what he could do to avert disaster. He was just entering the Shoreham Hotel when he met Senator Henderson, of Missouri, who had been one of his fellow delegates at the conference. As they talked, Henderson glanced across the street and said, "There's the President beckoning to you."

In those days our Presidents walked about, whenever and wherever they pleased, without even a one-man bodyguard.

Carnegie crossed the street and shook hands with the President.

"Hello, Carnegie," said he. "When did you arrive?"

"Just now. I was just going into the hotel to register."

"What are you here for?"

"To have a talk with you."

"Well, come along," said Mr. Harrison, taking his arm, "and talk as we walk."

They strolled the streets for an hour as dusk fell over the city, and the discussion was lively.

"Mr. President," said Carnegie, "that peace conference was practically a failure, but it is still our duty, I think, to be patient and forgiving. You remember you assured the Latin-American delegates that you put on that little military review in their honor to show them, not that we have an army, but rather that we have none and need none. You told them that ours is just the big brother in the family of American republics, and that all disputes, if any arise, will be settled by peaceful arbitration. I am surprised and grieved to find you taking a different course."

"But this isn't a mere dispute or difference of opinion," protested the President. "Our citizens have been wantonly killed and wounded. We have a reputation for protecting our citizens in foreign lands."

"When it comes to that, Mr. President," Carnegie retorted, "most of those sailors were not American citizens; they were foreigners. I am sorry to hear you are thinking of taking harsh measures against a little nation like Chile— over a street brawl."

"You New Yorkers think of nothing but business and

dollars!" exclaimed the President peevishly. "That is the way with New Yorkers; they think of their moneybags before the dignity and honor of the Republic."

"Mr. President," said Carnegie slowly and impressively, "I am one of the men in the United States who would profit most by war. As I am the largest manufacturer of steel, war might throw millions into my pockets."

"Well, that is probably true in your case," admitted Mr. Harrison.

"And if I were going to fight, I would pick on someone my size."

"Would you let any nation insult and dishonor you just because of its small size?"

"No man can dishonor me except myself," retorted Carnegie. "Honor wounds must be self-inflicted."

"You'd see our sailors attacked on shore and two of them killed, and you would stand that?"

"Mr. President, I do not think the United States is dishonored by a row among drunken sailors. I would be disposed to fire the captain of that ship for allowing the sailors to go ashore when the public peace was disturbed and there was already rioting in the town."

Darkness had fallen when they finally parted at the door of the White House. "I am going out to dinner tonight," said the President, "but come and dine with me tomorrow evening. There will be only the family here, and we can talk at length."

127

Next morning Carnegie called at the office of Secretary of State Blaine, who greeted him warmly.

"Why didn't we know you were here last night?" he asked. "When the President told Mrs. Blaine you were in the city, she lamented, 'Just think, Mr. Carnegie in town and I had a vacant seat that he could have occupied!' "

"I'm sorry to have missed the dinner," said Carnegie, "but I think it's rather fortunate that I didn't see you"— and he told of his discussion with Mr. Harrison.

"Yes, I suppose it was fortunate after all," agreed the Secretary. "The President might have thought you and I were in collusion."

While they were chatting, Senator Elkins of West Virginia came in. He laughed at seeing the caller. "I've just left the President," he remarked. "He tells me he had a long talk with you on the subject of Chile last evening, and that you came down hot and heavy on him about it. 'I know Mr. Carnegie feels very keenly on the subject of peace,' I told the President. 'If he was so emphatic with you, I'd like to hear what he'd say to me. He wouldn't speak as plainly to you as he would to me, you know. He would naturally be somewhat reserved in talking to you.' At that the President said, 'I didn't see the slightest indication of reserve, I assure you.' "

Thereupon both Blaine and Elkins laughed heartily.

At dinner the next evening the subject was discussed again, but in milder terms. Carnegie saw that the President's irritation was cooling a bit. He also noticed that the Executive was not looking well.

"Forgive me for mentioning it, Mr. President," said he, "but you look tired. You need a rest. Why don't you get away somewhere for a little vacation?"

"I had intended going out on a revenue cutter for a few days," replied Mr. Harrison, "but Justice Bradley of the Supreme Court died recently, you know, and—among other chores—I am trying to find a worthy successor to him."

"There is a man in Pittsburgh," said Carnegie, "whom I would recommend for the vacancy if he and I were not old fishing companions, and such close friends that you might suspect me of being unduly prejudiced in his favor. Perhaps I am too close a friend to judge him fairly, but I do know that he is a very learned and very upright jurist. Don't take my word for it. Investigate him."

"His name?"

"George Shiras."

The President nodded. "I know something of him. I'll take your advice and look him up."

He did so, and that is how one eminent justice of the Supreme Court came to be appointed. Meanwhile the Chilean squabble quieted and was settled amicably, and Carnegie had the satisfaction of believing that he had contributed something toward international peace. He had had quite a useful visit to Washington.

11

Homestead and Skibo

MORE AND MORE TIGHTLY ANDREW CARNEGIE HAD BEEN clamping down his policy of investing the Carnegie corporations' money in nothing but iron, steel, and the essentials which go into their making; that is, coal, coke, and iron ore. As he was driving into Pittsburgh one morning with Henry Phipps, they passed the place of business of a trust company whose name struck a chord in Carnegie's memory. Vaguely he recalled a warning phrase connected with it: "Stockholders individually liable."

"Didn't I notice on our books," he asked Phipps, "twenty shares of the stock of that concern as among our assets?"

"Yes," was the reply.

"Well, I wish you would sell those shares before you return to the office this afternoon."

"Oh, all right," agreed Phipps carelessly. "But there's no such hurry. It can be done any time."

"No, Harry," said the chief firmly. "Oblige me by doing it immediately."

When that bank failed a few months later with an enormous deficit, he felt amply justified. In 1888 the mills and furnaces were producing two thousand tons of steel and iron a day. The coke plants had five thousand ovens and they were turning out six thousand tons of coke a day. Their Frick Coke Company controlled forty-two thousand acres of that fine Connellsville coking-coal land. And through Harry Oliver, his boyhood friend, Carnegie obtained leases on a large acreage of the newly discovered Missabe iron-ore land in Minnesota. Their business was also extended by the establishment of a plant where hundreds of smaller steel articles were made, though even this seemed to "A. C." to be a little out of their line.

Carnegie himself had never had any serious trouble with labor. He maintained direct contact with the workmen, called most of their leaders by their first names, listened reasonably to their complaints, and corrected frictions and injustices. But as the vast group of Carnegie companies grew larger, new men and influences were coming into both management and labor. During Carnegie's long absences in Scotland every summer, discordances began to appear and grow. Now the loss of Tom Carnegie and Bill Jones—both of them wise, kind, and steadying influences—was deeply felt. Frick, who had become chairman

131

of the board of managers, proved to be a hard and ruthless man. Henry Phipps, as his years increased, began to lean toward Frick's views.

A small group of "heaters" and "rollers" at the Homestead plant was making trouble. The superintendent, who had recently come up from the ranks, showed poor judgment in dealing with the discontented ones, and the ill feeling spread to others. Charles Schwab, who had risen through management of the Braddock works to high station in the organization, was not in a position to negotiate at Homestead. And so in the summer of 1892 a strike was called at the Homestead plant, though a minority of the three thousand workmen were involved. Frick and the plant superintendent, encouraged by Carnegie's absence in Scotland, decided to employ strikebreakers—a violation of one of the principles dearest to their president's heart; one which he had already put in writing: "My idea is that the Company should be known as determined to let the men at any works stop work; that it will confer freely with them and wait patiently until they decide to return to work, never thinking of employing new men—never!"

The strikers, hearing rumors of Frick's intention, armed themselves and picketed the plant and the surrounding streets in force. Frick employed a large detective agency to act with the county sheriff and his deputies in protecting the strikebreakers as they entered the works. As the streets were blockaded by the strikers, an attempt was made on July the first to bring the new men, under guard, up the Monongahela River in boats, and thence into the rear of the mills. The result was a furious gun battle in which many were killed and wounded on each side, and the invaders were driven off.

Both factions were somewhat frightened at what they had done, and a compromise was therefore easier to arrive at. Carnegie, in Scotland, did not hear of the riot until two days later; then he cabled the officials that he would start homeward on the first ship available. Both Frick and Phipps promptly replied, telling him that the welfare of the company required that he remain away from America at this time. Though he couldn't comprehend the reason for it, he obeyed their injunction. He was deeply touched by a cable he received from the officers of the workmen's union after the battle: "Tell us what you wish us to do and we shall do it for you." But it was too late: the damage had been done. Phipps admitted to a New York newspaper twelve years later that he and Frick didn't want Carnegie present because they "knew of his extreme disposition always to grant the demands of labor, however unreasonable"—they wanted to handle the matter in their own way.

Years later Carnegie wrote in his autobiography of this affair: "Nothing I have ever had to meet in my life, before or since, wounded me so deeply. No pangs remain of any wound received in my business career save that of Homestead."

When he returned to America in the autumn, he went to the works and talked to some of the older men who had not been involved in the riot. "If you had been here," they told him, "the strike wouldn't have happened." When he said that he thought the offer of the company had been fair, one of the men replied. "Oh, Mr. Carnegie, it wasn't a question of dollars. The boys would have let you kick 'em, but they wouldn't even let that other man stroke their hair."

However, many people in America thought he showed cowardice in not returning at once when he heard of the trouble. His critics held it against him forever after.

He continued to take young men from the organization as partners—on his favorite terms—until there were more than thirty of them; each owned what sounds like an infinitesimal bit of stock, but it meant wealth to the possessor. To one of these, a young Scotsman named Alexander Peacock, he introduced the subject by saying, "Peacock, what would you give to be made a millionaire?"

"A liberal discount for cash, sir," was the prompt reply, which tickled his chief enormously.

On March 30, 1897, the Carnegies' only child was born— a pretty little girl. As her father first looked upon her, his wife said, "Her name is Margaret, after your mother. Now I have one request to make."

"What is it, Lou?" he asked.

"We must get a summer home, since this little one has been given us. We cannot rent one and be obliged to go in and out at a certain date. It should be our own home."

He readily agreed.

"I make only one condition," she went on.

"What is that?"

"It must be in the Highlands of Scotland."

She couldn't have suggested anything that would please him better. They could no longer have Cluny Castle for the summer, anyhow, because The Macpherson was about to be married and wanted the castle for his own use. But in the ten summers of their residence there, he and the Carnegies had become very close friends. They cabled him immediately the news of the baby's birth, and a great celebration took place in the Macpherson country—with nine big bonfires by night on as many hills, and much feasting and health-drinking.

So, instead of looking for another manor to lease, the new father now began seeking a property to buy. He found that the Duke of Sutherland had an estate named Skibo in the northern Scottish hill country which he was willing to sell. It appeared to have everything: forests, rugged beauty, delightful walks and climbs, good fishing, and an almost unbelievably equable climate—some flowering shrubs bloomed there in January. Best of all was a big old stone castle on a rocky eminence overlooking an estuary. Carnegie fell in love with Skibo at sight. He bought it; enlarged and remodeled the castle; installed an elevator, electric lights, up-to-date plumbing, even Turkish baths! There was a sanitary dairy, with the finest of stock; and the flower gardens became famous.

The castle was large enough to accommodate all the guests the Carnegies pleased to entertain at once—and there was a plenty of them! Some of the older friends, such as Gladstone and Matthew Arnold, were gone; but later ones—including Rudyard Kipling and Paderewski; Sir Edward Grey and Sir Charles Tennant, a Scotch steel manufacturer; Elihu Root and others—were coming on to fill the ranks. Their old and dear friends Lord and Lady Morley might come up two or three times in a season, and there were always the Dunfermline kin. At the railroad station, ten miles distant, guests were met by an old-fashioned, four-horse early Victorian coach—trim and glistening with new varnish—driven by a red-coated coachman, while a red-coated footman, high up on a rear seat, tooted a horn.

The Laird of Skibo scorned a family tree and a coat of arms; but he designed a Carnegie plaid, and wore the kilted tartan himself when he was at Skibo—as did little Margaret, frisking about the place or walking and climbing hand-in-hand with her father. The menservants and laborers on the estate wore it, too. The cloth was woven on cottage looms in the neighborhood. Scottishness was emphasized. The piper, who greeted the morning and who strode to and fro in the dining hall playing old Highland airs before dinner, was one of the most important persons on the place—as were a Scotch housekeeper, a Scotch butler, and a Scotch underservant or two. All of them went over to America with the family for the winters and, like the workmen on the estate, held their jobs for life.

On the Fourth of July both the American and the British flags floated over the castle, until that summer when a single flag was hoisted from the tower—one which at first puzzled the guests. Staring at it closely, they solved the problem: it was their host's unique combination of the flags of Britain and America—an expression, perhaps unintentional, of his hope that Great Britain and the United States would someday be welded into one great republic.

He could never bear to see wild animals killed. Deer, rabbits, and wild fowl were numerous on the estate, but he never hunted. He and his guests went fishing, for somehow fish didn't touch his sympathies as did land animals. But to guests who brought their guns and asked if they might hunt, he said, "Go shooting if you like. If you must kill them, kill them. But please don't let me know anything about it." Naturally, few guests cared to do any hunting under such circumstances. Bloodshed, whether of animals or of human beings, was abhorrent to Carnegie.

Meanwhile he was steadily giving away money to small colleges, buying organs for churches and synagogues, fostering symphony orchestras, building libraries. Every village within ten miles of Skibo—and some villages even farther away—has a Carnegie library. He gave $750,000 each to Cooper Institute and the Merchants and Tradesmen's Institution in New York, and $600,000 as a starter to Tuskegee Institute. Clinging fondly to old friendships, he pensioned men who had served under him on the Pittsburgh Division of the Pennsylvania Railroad from 1859 to 1863. Some of them had applied to him for aid, and finally he deputized his old friend Tom Miller to search for the others and put all that could be found—or their widows—on the pension list. "I was only a boy when I first went among these men," he explained. "They were very kind to me. They are dear friends." And as Miller sent in his reports on each, he wrote comments on many of them: "How well I remember John!" . . . "Bill was one of our best trackmen." . . . "Give my good wishes to Henry."

He was also deeply interested in the Civil War army telegraphers, with whom he had a bond of memory. He was a member of the historical association which they had organized, and sometimes attended one of their annual gatherings and told of his early days as a messenger boy. He was angered by the persistent failure of the government—despite all efforts in their behalf—to pension these men whose work had been so vital to the armies. Many of them risked their lives on the battlefield, just as had the soldiers; some of them were crippled or broken in health by wounds, exposure, or confinement in enemy prisons. Finally he set up his own fund for them, paying them pensions such as they should have been receiving from their country's government.

The following is but one example of Carnegie's ready and unfailing kindness to individuals in peculiar need.

Mr. Gladstone once said to him, "Our friend Lord Acton is in financial straits, and I am much concerned about him. You know what a fine library he has; you have seen it. Well, he is thinking of selling it—though he probably won't get what it is worth, and it will almost break his heart to part with it."

"I would buy it myself," said Carnegie, "if—"

"Let me make a suggestion," interrupted Gladstone. "Why don't you buy it and leave it with him for his lifetime, which I don't think will be long. Then you can do what you please with it."

"I'll do that!" exclaimed Carnegie, shaking hands with the statesman. "And thanks for the suggestion."

He bought the library at Acton's own price; but, as

Gladstone had predicted, the grateful peer did not live long to enjoy it. Carnegie and Morley were together shortly after his death in 1902. "I have something to tell you," said Carnegie to his friend. "You may remember that Lord Acton was in difficulties a few years ago, and proposed to sell his library—"

A knowing smile on Morley's face halted the sentence. "I must tell you," said he, "that I have known about this since the day you bought it."

"You have!"

"Yes, Gladstone couldn't keep the secret; he was so overjoyed because Lord Acton had it secure for life."

"Well," said Carnegie, "now I am going to hand it over to you."

"To me!" It was Morley's turn to be astonished.

"Yes. You will know how to make the best use of it; and I will trust you, when you pass away, to turn it over to some institution which will keep it together and cherish it."

12

Crisis and Solution

CARNEGIE KNEW THAT FRICK WAS ALWAYS HOPING TO GET some Carnegie stock into the hands of outsiders—of brokers, in fact, to be floated on the stock market. Finally, when Frick proposed to the company treasurer that he finance some improvements by selling two per cent of the company's stock to a multimillionaire Pittsburgh banker, and when he topped this by flatly violating a verbal agreement with Carnegie regarding the price of coke, the usually calm Scotchman really got mad.

What hurt Carnegie most of all was that Henry Phipps was siding with Frick. He came home, grim-faced, in the fall of 1899, determined to oust Frick from the company. There had never been any serious trouble among the partners before, and Carnegie detested the action he must take. He suggested that Frick sell his stock to other partners and retire peacefully from the company, but Frick refused.

141

It took a costly lawsuit and a compromise to get him out, but he finally went. Phipps made overtures of peace to Carnegie soon afterward and they became friendly once more, though their feeling toward each other was never again quite the same as in years past. As for Frick, he disliked Carnegie forever after for thwarting his schemes— though he lived and died a millionaire many times over.

The struggle had wearied Carnegie, and he began to yearn for freedom from business cares—and yet he couldn't endure the idea of leaving his lifework behind. The Morgan banking house, headed by the mighty J. Pierpont Morgan, was beginning to buy into the steel business. The Carnegie organization, of which Schwab was then president, retaliated by building a new steel plant at Conneaut, Ohio, on the shore of Lake Erie, where their Missabe ore could be delivered directly by boat.

Morgan now began to wonder whether Carnegie could be bought out. John W. Gates, whose barbed-wire and steel businesses he had taken over, said to him, "There is only one man who has influence with Carnegie, and that is Charlie Schwab. If you can enlist him, maybe you can put it over."

Morgan called Schwab and some other prominent steel men into consultation—a memorable conference which lasted all night.

"Yes, he is getting tired of the weight of business cares,"

said Schwab to them. "And yet I think he will fight the idea of cutting all connection with steel." But after some hours of discussing prices and plant-values, Schwab promised, "I'll see what I can do."

He very shrewdly approached Mrs. Carnegie first.

"I wish he would retire," she agreed. "I know he has turned the idea over in his mind at times, and yet he hates the thought of being out of it all."

They discussed it awhile, and presently she said, "Why don't you take him out for a golf game, and propose it to him while he's having a good time?" And she added with a smile, "If anybody can sell him the idea, you can, Charlie."

So Charlie Schwab took the boss up to a golf club in Westchester County, and broached the topic to him while they were trudging from green to green. At first he was cold to the subject. "No! No!" he said impatiently. "I don't want to retire." But his very impatience showed that he was fighting a battle within himself, and he was now besieged by the man whom his contemporaries have called the greatest salesman in history—a man whose personal charm and persuasiveness were almost irresistible.

"Morgan has hundreds of millions to put into the business," Schwab went on, "and he will build up opposition that will make it plenty tough for us. On the other hand, he will pay you almost anything you ask—"

143

"What does that matter?" protested Carnegie. "I don't need money. No, no, Charlie! What would I do with myself if I were out of business?"

"You could have a lot of fun giving away money," retorted Schwab. "You could begin to carry out that 'gospel of wealth' of yours"—and so he continued to pour it on, while his chief fell silent.

At length Carnegie asked, "What do the other partners think of this? Have you consulted them?"

"Three or four of us have mentioned it to one another in a casual way," admitted Schwab. "That's all. But I'm sure they will all be willing. You see, those of us who want to stay in the steel business will accept stock and bonds of the new United States Steel Corporation, which Morgan proposes to organize. You could have bonds, which you could readily convert into cash or use for endowments."

Carnegie said little more until just before they parted for the afternoon. Then, "See the other partners, and find out what they think about it," he directed.

The other partners were all in agreement as to the sale, and Schwab so notified Morgan. The banker then called Carnegie by telephone, and after they had exchanged greetings he brought up the all-important subject. "Why don't you come down and talk it over?" he suggested.

"Mr. Morgan," retorted the Steel King sweetly, "it's just

as far from Fifty-first Street to Wall Street as it is from Wall to Fifty-first."

Morgan caught the implication at once. The world's largest steelmaker wasn't going to be patronized by the world's largest banker. Steel was bigger than money; the mountain must come to Mahomet.

"I'll come up," growled Morgan.

He called a hack and drove up to the Carnegie home, and in fifteen minutes the gigantic transaction was agreed upon. As they talked, Carnegie wrote the figures "$400,000,000" on a slip of paper and handed it to the caller. That was the sales price of his own interest.

Morgan's granite countenance did not change in the slightest degree. "That is satisfactory," he said, and after a few more words he got into the hack and returned to Wall Street. He told Schwab later, "I would have given him a hundred million more if he had asked for it."

So Morgan organized the United States Steel Corporation with $1,100,000,000 capital stock, and Charles M. Schwab—who twenty-five years before had been a teenage stagecoach driver in the Pennsylvania hills—as president. Charlie's old chief thought approvingly that the business couldn't have been placed in more capable hands.

The letdown feeling which followed Carnegie's relinquishment of his business interests did not last long. Soon he began to think of the many things he wanted to do.

Charlie was right: he was going to have a lot of fun giving away his fortune. He was sixty-six years old, and there might not be much time left.

True, he had not paused in his giving. A dumpy little figure with a round, genial, kindly, white-bearded face, this man who had set himself the task of giving away $400,000,000 would have been the ideal personification of Santa Claus if his beard had been longer. But for thousands of schools, colleges, churches, charities, and individuals that he had aided without the desire for any return, he was already the embodiment of Santa Claus.

Even now he was negotiating with the trustees of the New York Public Library for the building of numerous branch libraries; and in the preceding year he had founded the Carnegie Institute of Technology at Pittsburgh with an initial gift of a million dollars, to which he continued to add until it reached $16,000,000 in his lifetime. There were four units in the plant which was built in Schenley Park: Schools of Applied Science, Applied Design, Applied Industries, and the Margaret Morrison Carnegie School—which offered courses in domestic science and allied subjects to young women—all leading to Bachelor of Science degrees.

One of the first things Carnegie did upon retirement was to set aside $5,000,000 for the benefit of employees of the steel works and furnaces—a million of this amount for the maintenance of the libraries he had established for them; the remainder for old-age pensions, for the aid of men injured in the works, and for the benefit of the families of workmen who might be killed.

In the spring he went over to Scotland to be installed as the Lord Rector of St. Andrews, the oldest and proudest of the four Scotch universities. The Lord Rector had once been a high official in these institutions; but, as the centuries passed, the post had become an honorary one, always held by some distinguished man who was elected yearly by the students. Carnegie was justifiably proud of the honor of being one of the long roster of eminent men who had occupied this position during the five centuries of St. Andrews' history—and the first who was not a British subject. He was prouder still when the students re-elected him in the following year, 1902, for another term.

He greatly enjoyed the "Rector's Nights," when the students had him to themselves for give-and-take—no member of the faculty was permitted to be present. After the first Rector's Night, Principal Donaldson told him that the students had said, "Rector So-and-so talked *to* us; Rector Thus-and-so talked *at* us—both from the platform. Mr. Carnegie sat down in our circle and talked *with* us"—and as there were only about two hundred students, this wasn't hard to do.

Finding that the four institutions—Aberdeen, Edinburgh,

Glasgow, and St. Andrews—were all more or less straitened financially, and that there were many boys of ability who couldn't afford a college course, Carnegie set up the Scottish Universities Trust—a $10,000,000 fund, one-half of which was for the benefit of the four institutions themselves, the other half for the aid of worthy youth desirous of securing an education. The Carnegies invited the university principals, together with their families, to spend a week at Skibo. Also present were the Earl of Elgin, chairman of the Universities Trust, and Lord Balfour, Secretary for Scotland in the British Cabinet. Thereafter, "Principals' Week" became an annual event at Skibo, and was always a happy occasion.

At the end of the first Principals' Week, Principal Lang, shaking Carnegie's hand in departure, said, "It has taken the principals of the Scottish universities five hundred years to learn how to begin our sessions. Spending a week together is the solution."

Now that he was a free lance, the retired industrialist was pleasantly surprised to find how much there was that he wanted to do. One item was to collect some of the essays he had been writing for American and British magazines, and publish them, with additional material, in 1901 in a volume entitled *The Empire of Business*. He began playing with the idea of a biography of James Watt, too. And there was a new home to be built, two miles farther up Fifth Avenue, between Ninetieth and Ninety-first streets. The family moved into it in 1902. It was large but—like its builder—sturdy, square, and simple in design, and the grounds surrounding it were bright with flowers from spring to autumn. In the master's modest bedroom there was only one picture hanging on the wall—a portrait of Bill Jones.

When the Carnegie corporations passed out of existence, the partners—forty-three in number—organized the Carnegie Veterans' Association to keep alive the memory of the old days until the last of them died. Upon completion of the new home, Mrs. Carnegie, to her husband's delight, said, "Let's have the veterans first." So they came, for the dinner-housewarming; and thereafter the veterans' dinner was an annual event eagerly looked forward to by all—especially by the host, who considered it one of the chief joys of the year. "My Boys," Carnegie called them, and as he felt their evident affection for him—saw it glowing in their eyes—he wrote in his autobiographical notes: "Rather this, minus fortune, than multimillionairedom without it; yes, a thousand times, yes!"

At the first of the dinners Mrs. Carnegie was elected an honorary member of the Veterans' Association. Then someone proposed, "Let's elect little Margaret too"—which they promptly did.

It wasn't long before one of the veterans—Charles

Schwab, the once-poor country boy, now head of the so-called "Steel Trust"—erected a massive home on Riverside Drive—a huge, pinnacled structure patterned after the châteaux along the River Loire, in the France he so dearly loved.

"Have you seen Charlie's new mansion?" his old boss would sometimes ask a friend, with a chuckle. "By comparison it makes my house look like a cottage."

13

──

Distribution

THE DIRECTOR OF THE NEW YORK PUBLIC LIBRARY, MR. J. S. Billings—who had been negotiating with Carnegie for a number of branch libraries in the boroughs of Manhattan and the Bronx—calmly suggested in 1901 that he build sixty-five branches at a cost of $80,000 each—a total of $5,200,000, exclusive of incidental expenses.

"Five and a quarter millions is a pretty large order," said Carnegie, "but if the buildings are needed, they must be built." So the city set about acquiring the sites, and the work went forward as rapidly as possible—with no delays for lack of funds, as there so often are when there is no industrial Aladdin to produce the cash. And that wasn't all the money that was needed, either. Three more buildings were added to the original estimate, and then the Brooklyn Public Library—a separate organization—was given twenty branches. For all these libraries there were certain requisites: each must have a reference and a circulation department, a children's room, and a file of magazines; in outward appearance every building must be recognizable as a library, yet no two could be exactly alike.

Not the least useful feature of many of the buildings was a little basement theater where plays were sometimes presented, and where night classes in English and other subjects were held in later years. For several years a philanthropic New York theatrical producer, John Golden, maintained what he called the Library Theater, employing excellent companies of professional actors to tour these little theaters and present good plays recently seen on Broadway. Admission was free of charge, to a selected list of library patrons.

By 1919, when his benefactions ceased forever, Carnegie had given 2,811 free public library buildings, costing $60,364,808. Of these, 1946 were in the United States; the rest, in foreign countries. The usefulness of these libraries—the information and pleasure they have given to millions upon millions of human beings—is incalculable.

"The fundamental advantage of a library," the giver himself said, "is that it gives nothing for nothing. Youths must acquire knowledge themselves. There is no escape from this." And he went on: "It was from my own early experience that I decided there was no use to which money could be applied so productive of good to boys and girls who had good within them and ability and ambition to develop it, as the founding of a public library in a community which is willing to support it as a municipal institution. I am sure that the future of those libraries I have been privileged to found will prove the correctness of this opinion. For if one child in each library district, by having access to one of these libraries, is half as much benefited as I was by having access to Colonel Anderson's four hundred well-worn volumes, I shall consider they have not been established in vain."

Even while the New York libraries were being created, the foundation of the Carnegie Institution of Washington was under way—its actual birthday was January 28, 1902. To this its creator gave $25,000,000 "to encourage investigation, research and discovery, and the application of knowledge to the improvement of mankind." John Hay, Secretary of State under Theodore Roosevelt, was the first chairman of the board. Besides its Economic Sociology, Historical Research, and Geophysical departments at Washington, the Institution has several activities elsewhere: a botanical laboratory on the Arizona desert; a marine biological laboratory on the Dry Tortugas Islands, off the coast of Florida; the Mount Wilson Observatory, with its great telescope, in California; an observatory at Albany, N. Y.; a small ship which sails the oceans correcting earlier surveys and maps—and these are not all.

153

Next Carnegie took up what was to become one of his favorite causes—the Hero Fund Commission, which he launched in 1904 with a $5,000,000 grant. His thought was turned in this direction by a tragic accident in a coal mine near Pittsburgh. Men were entombed in the pit by an explosion; and a former superintendent of the mine—a Mr. Taylor, who had gone into another business—drove hastily to the scene, hoping that his experience and knowledge of that particular mine might be of service. At the head of a party of volunteers, who rallied eagerly to his well-known leadership, he led the way down the shaft. They succeeded in rescuing many of the survivors, but the brave Taylor lost his life.

"Greater love hath no man than this, that a man lay down his life for his friends." The words haunted Carnegie for days after the disaster, and in no great while the Hero Fund was born. "I cherish a fatherly regard for it," he wrote later, "since no one suggested it to me. As far as I know, it had never been thought of; hence it is emphatically 'my ain bairn.'"

As it was intended to apply only to the heroes and heroines of peacetime, not of war, some persons were doubtful of its merits. These critics falsely assumed that its purpose was to stimulate heroic action—to induce people to perform deeds of daring for the sake of reward. Of course such an idea never entered the donor's head.

"True heroes think not of reward," wrote Carnegie. "They are inspired and think only of their fellows endangered; never of themselves."

The commission acts only after a searching investigation of instances brought to its attention. Those who have been injured "in heroic effort to save human life" are aided financially until again able to work. In case of death, the widow and children, or other dependents, are provided for "until she remarries, and the children until they reach a self-supporting age." Even if the hero is uninjured, a sum of money may be given if the commission considers such a gift desirable. A medal reciting the heroic deed it commemorates is given to the hero, or widow, or next of kin.

The chairmanship of the Hero Fund Commission fell upon a former Carnegie partner, Charles Taylor—who, by the way, was not related to the man whose self-sacrifice had prompted the establishment of the fund. Taylor was already in charge of the relief fund for former steel-mills workmen, and the fund for Pennsylvania Railroad men who had worked under Carnegie long ago. So now he was administering three pension funds, zealously and efficiently, avoiding publicity and refusing to accept a cent of pay for any of the work. Naturally his old chief's affection for such a man was very deep. When Taylor, who was a loyal alumnus of Lehigh University, began pointing out to Carnegie that the university needed a new laboratory,

"Aha!" thought the philanthropist. "Here is where I get even with Charlie."

He wrote to President Drinker of Lehigh, offering the money for a laboratory building if the trustees would permit him to name it. "Certainly!" was the reply, and the donor specified "Taylor Hall." Sometime later, Charlie came to Carnegie, flustered with embarrassment.

"This won't do, Mr. Carnegie," he protested. "I'm not donating the building and I'm not a person of prominence; I'm just a modest alumnus. I've done nothing to merit such an honor."

"You sold me the idea," interrupted Carnegie. "You pestered me half to death until I offered the money for the building. I say nothing of your having headed three of my pet projects, and worked like a nailer at them without accepting a cent of pay."

"Of course I wouldn't accept pay for such little chores," returned Taylor. "If you can give millions of money for such things, I can certainly give a few hours' time. It isn't that; it's the idea of having a university building named for an obscurity. It'll make me ridiculous, when everybody knows I didn't pay for the building. When strangers see that name over the door, they'll ask, 'Who in the heck is or was Taylor?'"

Putting his hands in his pockets, Carnegie leaned back in his chair until Charlie had blown off steam and run out of words. Then he came back at him, shaking a finger, "Maybe it will make you ridiculous if I insist upon Taylor Hall, though I deny it. But you ought to be willing to make such sacrifice for Lehigh. If you weren't consumed with vanity, you wouldn't care how much your name is used if it helps your Alma Mater. Taylor isn't much of a name, anyhow. It's your insufferable vanity that's making all the trouble. You should conquer it—"

"Oh, now, stop your kidding, chief," protested Taylor, red-faced. "You're distorting the question; you know it."

"Well, you can make your decision," said Carnegie with a wave of the hand. "You can sacrifice the name of Taylor or you can sacrifice Lehigh, just as you like; but 'No Taylor, no Hall'—that's the ultimatum, Charlie."

Taylor finally threw up his hands in surrender.

"Visitors who may look upon that structure in after days," wrote Carnegie, "and wonder who Taylor was, may rest assured that he was a loyal son of Lehigh, a working, not merely a preaching, apostle of the gospel of service to his fellow man, and one of the best men that ever lived."

The original Hero Fund Commission covered only the United States, Canada, and Newfoundland. But in 1908 Carnegie established a Hero Fund for Great Britain and Ireland; and later he did the same for Germany, Belgium, the Netherlands, France, Sweden, Norway, Switzerland, Italy, and Denmark, receiving personal letters of appreciation from King Edward VII of Great Britain, Kaiser Wilhelm II of Germany, and numerous other high-ranking personages.

For several years he endowed one big foundation every year, with much golden largess in between: more than $2,000,000 for the Church Peace Union; $1,500,000 toward the building of the great Peace Palace at The Hague; $850,000 to the International Bureau of American Republics—besides church organs, libraries, college buildings, laboratories, professorships. Some of the tight-minded old Highland Scotch Presbyterians, who had always regarded musical instruments in churches as "irreleegious," grumbled that Andra Carnegie was demoralizing Christian worship by putting organs into churches; the human voice was the only pious music—not a "kist-full of whistles." After hearing much of this talk, Carnegie wrote to Scotland: "I am so affected by it that I feel I must have a partner in my sin. Hereafter I am going to ask a congregation to pay half the cost of the organ." That reduced the demand for organs in the Scottish Highlands.

He liked to christen his gifts to colleges with the name of some person whom he admired, or whose friendship or memory was dear to him. Among such were the John Hay Library at Brown University, the Elihu Root Foundation at Hamilton College, the Hanna Chair at Western Reserve University, and the Frances Cleveland Library at

Wellesley. The Stanton Chair of Economics at Kenyon College in Ohio was founded in memory of Edwin M. Stanton, President Lincoln's Secretary of War, who was known to most people as rough and surly, but whom the Steel King remembered best as the Pittsburgh lawyer who was always genial and kind to a little telegraph messenger boy named Andy Carnegie.

One of his best-loved philanthropies was that which endowed his native town of Dunfermline, giving it a long-coveted park and its old historic buildings. Among Andrew's earliest recollections were the stories his elders told of the long struggle of their townspeople to obtain possession of, or certain rights in, their ancient heritage—the old Abbey and its grounds, and the Palace ruins—which for generations had been in the possession of the Hunts, the Lairds of Pittencrieff. Included in the contested area was Pittencrieff Glen, a lovely, rocky, wooded hollow of more than sixty acres bordered by the two main streets of the town. To little Andrew the Glen was so beautiful that he thought Paradise must resemble it. But he could only look at it from the outside, for he was barred from entering it. His Grandfather Morrison was a leader in the campaign against the Hunts, and his uncle Bailie Morrison not only led in a court battle but was accused of inciting a band of men to tear down a barrier which the Laird had erected. Thereupon the Laird ordered that no Morrison might be admitted to the

Glen—and the name Morrison included the Carnegie kin. So Uncle Lauder could only take Dod and Naig around the edge of the Glen on a Sunday afternoon, and to a certain high spot from which they could look down into it.

There came a time, around 1900, when Dr. John Ross of Dunfermline, who sometimes acted for Carnegie in charitable and other undertakings, said to him privately, "I have heard intimations that Colonel Hunt might sell his holdings in Dunfermline."

"Good!" exclaimed Carnegie. "I'll buy them."

"But the price he is asking is far too high, I think," objected Ross.

They discussed the matter further, and agreed that Dr. Ross should proceed to feel out the situation with true Scotch caution. In the autumn of 1902, after a year or more spent in verbal fencing, Dr. Ross came to call upon Carnegie.

"I thought we might let Mr. Shaw of Edinburgh"—a former Dunfermline man—"broach the subject to Colonel Hunt's agents," said he.

"Yes," said Carnegie, "intimate to them that their client may someday regret not closing with me. They may not so easily find another purchaser willing to buy, and there is also the possibility that I may change my mind—or pass away."

"Tom Shaw will know how to take care of it," said Ross.

The Carnegies sailed for New York shortly after that. Weeks went by, and one day there came a cable from Shaw: "Colonel Hunt will accept 45,000 pounds. Shall I close?"

To this, Carnegie replied: "Yes, provided it is under Ross's conditions."

A few days passed; then, late one afternoon—it was Christmas Eve—there came another cable from Shaw: "Hail, Laird of Pittencrieff!"

That told the story. "I couldn't have had a finer Christmas present!" cried the Laird. "I am the happy possessor of the grandest title on earth! The King—well, after all, he is only the King. He doesn't own King Malcom's tower, nor St. Margaret's shrine, nor Pittencrieff Glen. Not he, poor man. I do, and I shall be glad to show him around—condescendingly—should he ever visit Dunfermline."

In the deed to the trustees—headed, of course, by Dr. Ross—he said that his object was: "To bring into the monotonous lives of the toiling masses of Dunfermline more of "sweetness and light," to give to them—especially the young—some charm, some happiness, some elevating conditions of life which residence elsewhere would have denied, that the child of my native town, looking back in after years, however far from home it may have roamed, will feel that, simply by virtue of being such, life has been made happier and better.

He startled the trustees by handing them $2,500,000 with which to develop the property and establish a maintenance fund. Additional gifts later brought the total up to $3,750,000. No public property has ever been quite so well cared for; none has ever been dearer to its people.

As a trustee of Cornell University, Carnegie had become aware of the poor salaries paid to educators. "Of all professions," he exclaimed impatiently, "that of teaching is probably the most unfairly, yes, most meanly paid, though it should rank with the highest. Educated men, devoting their lives to teaching the young, receive mere pittances." So on April 16, 1905, he launched the Carnegie Foundation for the Advancement of Teaching, with a capital of $10,000,000 in five-per-cent bonds, to encourage higher education in the United States and Canada by providing retirement pay for university and college teachers, and pensions for their widows.

The board of trustees consisted of twenty-five university and college presidents, many of them already his friends; and when they met at the Carnegie home for organization, one of the thoughts that occurred to him was that now he would add to his list several new friends to be admired and cherished. He could never have too many friends.

Two years later he gave an additional $5,000,000 to the foundation, then $1,250,000 more, and in 1918 the Carnegie Corporation contributed $12,000,000. During its first

quarter-century the Fund distributed more than $20,000,-
000 in allowances and pensions to eleven hundred teachers
and five hundred widows. When Carnegie's foundation and
John D. Rockefeller's great General Education Board were
found to be duplicating each other's activities at times, Mr.
Rockefeller said, "Why don't you take a seat on our
board? Then you would know what is going on in both
agencies and could prevent overlapping." Carnegie agreed,
to the advantage of both funds.

Richard Watson Gilder, noted editor and critic and
close friend of Carnegie, once wrote of him: "A. C. is a
man of enormous faculty and great imagination. His views
are truly large and prophetic. And unless I am mistaken,
he has a genuine ethical character. He is not perfect, but
he is most interesting and remarkable; a true democrat, his
benevolent actions having a root in principal and character." And on another occasion: "A. C. is really a tre-
mendous personality—dramatic, wilful, generous, whimsi-
cal, at times almost cruel in pressing his own convictions
upon others, and then again, tender, affectionate, emo-
tional, always imaginative, unusual and wide-visioned in
his views. He is well worth Boswellizing, but I am urging
him to be his own Boswell. . . . He is inconsistent in many
ways, but with a passion for lofty views; the brotherhood
of man, peace among nations, religious purity . . ."

Carnegie may have been inconsistent, but he always

lived up to his convictions; yet he was seldom obstinate in his views. When he had organized one of his great trusts and explained its general purpose, he usually left the management of it to the discretion of the governing board. And he gave up many of his pet projects when persons whose opinions he respected convinced him that they were impracticable. Take, for example, the case of the Confederate bonds. In 1865, at the end of the Civil War, the defeated Confederate States of America were so utterly ruined financially and economically that they were forced to repudiate their government bonds, many of which were held in Europe. As the Southern states had later been readmitted to the Union, Carnegie—hoping to create a better feeling for us in Europe—once proposed to pay off all these bonds. But lawyers and financiers, as well as statesmen, convinced him that it would be difficult, if not impossible, to do so without creating more bitterness than good feeling, so he reluctantly gave up the thought.

In 1906, after a few years' interval, Carnegie was chosen for a third term as Lord Rector of St. Andrews. At the time of the Principals' Week that summer, the Carnegies had an American guest—Miss Agnes Irwin, Dean of Radcliffe College and a great-granddaughter of Benjamin Franklin. Principal Donaldson of St. Andrews was deeply impressed —as indeed were all the Scotch guests—to see this descendant of Franklin at Skibo, for St. Andrews had given him his first honorary degree, that of Doctor of Laws, in 1759.

Later that year, during the celebration at Philadelphia of the two hundredth anniversary of Franklin's birth, St. Andrews sent to Miss Irwin the same degree it had given her great-grandfather one hundred and forty-seven years before, and it deputized its incumbent Lord Rector, Andrew Carnegie, to confer the degree and place the hood on her shoulders.

Now "A. C." was beginning at odd moments to jot down paragraphs and chapters of his autobiography—reminding himself sadly of how many of the dear friends and kinsmen of whom he wrote were dead. "I couldn't bear to visit the steel mills now," he once said. "It would recall too many who have gone before. So few of my early friends would remain to give me the hand-clasp of the days of old. There would be only one or two of the old men still left who would call me 'Andy!'"

14

Late Afternoon

IN 1907 THE PEACE SOCIETY OF NEW YORK WAS ORGANIZED, with the hope that it might do something toward the gradual elimination of war. Knowing Andrew Carnegie's deep devotion to that cause, the society asked him to accept its presidency.

"No, no!" he said. "I'm with you, heart and soul—you know that—and I'll do all in my power to help you, but I'm too busy with other matters to take the presidency of the Peace Society. I would feel that I had to devote most of my time to it, and I can't do that."

But after the committee had gone away, his conscience troubled him. "Am I as busy as I think I am?" he asked himself. "What am I good for, anyhow? If I'm not willing to sacrifice myself for the cause of peace, for what would I sacrifice?"

Only a few days had passed when a group of men,

166

including some who had been there before, came to call, with Dr. Lyman Beecher at their head. Carnegie guessed their errand.

"Don't say a word," he greeted them. "I know what you're here for. My conscience has been tormenting me ever since I gave you that refusal the other day. Now I'm repentant. I'll accept your presidency and do my duty."

The following spring the society held a peace conference in New York which was attended by delegations from most of the states of the Union, as well as by many distinguished persons from foreign lands. But it became evident that something more than meetings and speeches and resolutions was needed to bring about peace among mankind. Having no other means that he could think of, Carnegie decided to use the most powerful tool he had—money. It was proving effective in carrying out his other aims; if spending it would bring peace, he would pour it out like water.

And so, on December 14, 1910, he launched his only project which has seemed to be a failure—the Carnegie Endowment for International Peace. As the head of its board of trustees he chose one of the men he admired most—Elihu Root—and he left the forming of a program entirely to the wisdom of the trustees.

They did what they could. They organized the activities under three divisions. The Division of Intercourse and Education maintains agencies throughout the world to gather information about international policies, and tries to promote international good will. It arranges for the exchange of eminent scholars and writers among nations, and aids peace organizations already existing. The Division of Economics and History studies the conditions—political, social, and economic—which influence peace and war, and suggests methods of action in regard to them. The Division of International Law tries to extend the law of nations —which, after all, is only a body of rules or agreements—to all disputes which may arise among nations.

Lord Morley thought that it took an incurable optimist to believe in the efficacy of his friend's Endowment for International Peace, and Carnegie was destined to learn by a sad object lesson that argument and propaganda alone cannot hasten the abolition of international war.

Carnegie believed that "we are drawn together because opposites are mutually beneficial to each other. I am optimistic, all my ducks being swans. He is pessimistic, looking out soberly, even darkly, upon the dangers ahead, and sometimes imagining vain things. The world seems bright to me, and earth is often a real heaven—so happy I am, and so thankful to the kind fates. Morley is seldom if ever wild about anything; his judgment is always deliberate and his eyes are ever seeing the spots on the sun."

Morley, on the other hand, liked his friend's optimism

and enthusiasm, even if he didn't always agree with it. Said he, "It is wiser to do justice to his spacious feel for the great objects of the world—for knowledge and its spread, invention, light, improvement of social relations, equal chances to the talents, the passion for peace. These are glorious things; a touch of exaggeration in expression is easy to set right."

Many countries honored Carnegie for having tried to bring about peace. The French government made him Knight Commander of the Legion of Honor; from Holland came the Grand Cross Order of Orange-Nassau; Denmark bestowed on him the Grand Cross Order of Dannebrog, and twenty-one American republics bestowed gold medals upon him. He received honorary doctorates from scores of universities and colleges, and he was a member of more than one hundred and ninety institutes, learned societies, and clubs.

He was writing his own will, and putting into it a provision for a trust fund intended to carry out a great scheme for the benefit of the American people. But when he chanced to mention this provision to Elihu Root one day, Root shook his head.

"Have you forgotten what you yourself said, years ago—that to try planning such a future operation in your will is a risky business, because it so often goes wrong either in practice or in the courts? Don't repeat the mistake of

Samuel J. Tilden. He tried to do with his fortune just what you are thinking of, and it was upset in court.

"Wills are pretty shaky vehicles," Root went on. "Why don't you organize your trust now, in your lifetime, and transfer to it the bulk of your fortune—what you have left of it—get the thing going nicely while you are still alive? Then you can not only be sure that it is working well, but you can have the pleasure of seeing it doing the things you want done."

He took Root's advice, and in 1911 the New York legislature chartered the Carnegie Corporation of New York with a capital of $25,000,000 in five-per-cent first-mortgage bonds of the United States Steel Corporation. The group of prominent men whom he had asked to serve as trustees met at his home on November 11 of that year, and he read to them his statement of the purpose of the trust: "To promote the advancement and diffusion of knowledge and understanding among the people of the United States, by aiding technical schools, institutions of higher learning, libraries, scientific research, hero funds, useful publications, and by such other agencies and means as shall from time to time be found appropriate therefor."

This trust was intended to contribute to any of his other foundations whenever they needed help, as well as to any other movement for intellectual and social progress in America. But he had no sooner established the Corporation than he began to see that its original endowment was insufficient. It would require more—far more—to do what he would like to see done. However, he was now down to the point where he had only $125,000,000 in bonds and cash to leave to his wife and daughter. Would they agree to his giving another fifty or a hundred millions to the Corporation? Mrs. Carnegie, without a moment's hesitation, said Yes; and to Margaret, then in her middle teens, whatever her beloved father did was satisfactory. So in 1912 the endowment of the Corporation was increased to $125,000,000. In one year the philanthropist had given away $130,403,000.

Carnegie had for years fretted over the failure of Congress to provide for our ex-Presidents and Presidents' widows. It seemed to him ungrateful and indecent to elevate them to the highest honors and the most strenuous and responsible position in the Republic, and then deny them the pensions which would enable them to pass the years of their retirement in dignity and freedom from worry. He proposed that the Corporation pay each of them $25,000 a year after they leave the White House, "as long as they remain unprovided for by the Government."

But when his plan became publicly known, there was a murmur of protest from many people. It was unfitting, they said, that a private citizen should take on an obligation which ought to be assumed by the Government. The truth was that it shamed them; they feared that it would humiliate the Nation in the eyes of the world. So Carnegie reluctantly dropped the idea—or, rather, he postponed it; for he never quite gave it up, as we shall see.

That winter of 1911-12 was saddened by the death of his boyhood chum Tom Miller. Only a few months before, Carnegie had written in his autobiography that he "still lives and sheds upon us the sweetness and light of a most lovable nature, a friend who grows more precious as the years roll by." Now Tom was gone, and another line was added: "Henceforth life lacks something, lacks much—my first partner in early years, my dearest friend in old age. May I go where he is, wherever that may be."

Whatever pride he may have felt in his great foundations and institutions, the benefaction dearest to his heart was his own private pension list. As might be expected, he received thousands of letters every year asking for financial aid. Naturally he had no means of knowing how many of the writers were impostors, how many of the stories were fictitious. But he pored through the correspondence and picked out many that seemed genuine, making notes on the letters to Poynton, his secretary: "Put him on for $50 a month," or "See that the old lady wants nothing to make her comfortable." Among those most certain to be included in his pension list were persons whom he had known in the long-ago, or who were connected by some tie of memory with his childhood or youth. A few of them had asked him for help, but most of them had either been mentioned to him by others or been sought for by himself. Among them were a daughter of the man who had given him his first job; a once-prosperous Pittsburgh merchant to whom little Andy had delivered telegrams, but who was now poor and decrepit; a fellow member of the old Swedenborgian choir in Allegheny; two old maiden ladies, because "I used to dance with them when I was a gay young man."

Aware that this list would require considerable sums of money as time went on—there were more than five hundred names on it before he died—Carnegie established a $5,000,000 endowment trust to assure payment of the benefits as long as the pensioners lived.

Of course there was a list in Scotland, too, with Dr. Ross of Dunfermline, now Sir John Ross, as trustee. Among the names found on it were those of a great-granddaughter of Robert Burns and a daughter of an old Dunfermline postman who had been a beloved friend of Carnegie's childhood.

One day Dr. Henry S. Pritchett, head of the Carnegie Corporation of New York, was asked to call at the Carnegie home. When he arrived, he found his host pacing the floor of the drawing room.

"Dr. Pritchett," said Carnegie, "I want to create a foundation for Great Britain similar to the one you head for America—on a much smaller scale, of course; I haven't the money left to give to it in such quantity, though, to be sure, it doesn't need as much. I don't want to take another ten millions away from my wife and my daughter's dowry, so I think I'll withdraw ten millions from your corporation's capital."

Dr. Pritchett looked uncomfortable. "But I don't think you can do that, Mr. Carnegie," said he.

"I can't?"

"No, I think your endowment of the Carnegie Corporation of New York is permanent, and cannot be altered."

Carnegie could hardly believe it. "Ask Mr. Root," said Dr. Pritchett. "I'm sure I'm right, but ask Root. He'll know."

He called up Root, then a Senator. "No, indeed," said the eminent authority. "You can't take money away from the Corporation now. What's done is done, and you can't change it."

That was a damper! He had his heart set on that British fund. He had assigned his remaining $25,000,000 in bonds to his wife and Margaret. But did they really need all that?

After long pondering, he explained the situation to Mrs. Carnegie. "Do you mind," he asked, "if I take ten millions of your bonds for this fund?"

She did not hesitate a moment. "Certainly not, Andrew," she replied with a smile, confirming for the thousandth time his opinion that there never had been and never would be another woman equal to her. And so the British Carnegie Fund was founded.

174

"How much have I given away now, Poynton?" he would sometimes ask his secretary. Poynton always had the figures ready, right on the tip of his tongue—"$347,285,500" (or whatever it was) he would reply.

"Good heavens!" with a chuckle. "Where on earth did I ever get all that money?"

On August 29, 1913, he stood in the Peace Palace at The Hague and voiced his belief that all that was required for the maintenance of world peace was "an agreement between three or four of the leading civilized powers (and as many more as desire to join) pledged to cooperate against disturbers of world peace, should such arise."

Eleven months later, on July 28, 1914, Austria declared war on Serbia. Carnegie's mind was wholly unprepared for such an event. He had met Kaiser Wilhelm II of Germany in 1907; had dined on his yacht and formed a high opinion of him, believing that he was earnestly anxious for the peace and progress of the world. Now, during the early days of World War I, Carnegie was at first startled and incredulous, then shocked and stricken with grief to the depths of his soul. As the vast extent of the horror became more apparent, he realized that all his labor and investment in behalf of peace had been in vain. All his dreams for a quiet and happy world were shattered!

The outbreak of war cut short the family's summer in Scotland. They hurried down to Liverpool to take a steamer for home, and there Morley came to see them off. When the two devoted friends clasped hands and said good-by, it was for the last time.

Thereafter Carnegie's strength and vitality slowly but steadily declined. The family spent the summer of 1915 at Bar Harbor, Maine, and the following summer at Noroton, Connecticut. After the United States entered the war, Carnegie created libraries for thirty-two American army cantonments. Early in 1917 he purchased an estate called Shadowbrook in the Berkshire Hills near Lenox, Massachusetts, and there his last three summers were spent. Charlie Schwab and Root and some other good friends came to call now and then. Tom Miller, Mark Twain, Richard Watson Gilder, John Bigelow, and Joseph Choate had died. Morley was still living, and the two friends wrote a short letter to each other every Sunday.

On April 22, 1919, Margaret—who only yesterday, it seemed, was a tiny girl toddling about the hills and glens of Skibo hand-in-hand with her father—was married to a fine young New Yorker, Roswell Miller, Jr. It was the last festivity of her father's life.

That summer George Lauder, Jr., came to visit at Shadowbrook, and the two took leisurely walks together, did some fishing, and played many games of checkers. Then Cousin Dod, too, said a last good-by.

Early in August, Carnegie was stricken with pneumonia. Mrs. Carnegie and the faithful valet—a Morrison, by the way—remained in constant attendance. On the second

176

day after the attack—it was a Sunday—for the first time in years, he did not write to Morley. That evening, though he was very weak, his condition seemed satisfactory. After saying good night his wife added, "I hope you will rest well, Andrew."

"I hope so, Lou," he replied.

Soon he fell into a deep, quiet sleep from which he never awoke.

He was buried not far from the resting place of Washington Irving, in Sleepy Hollow Cemetery, just north of Tarrytown, New York. Over his grave stands a tall Celtic cross of Scottish granite. The tenant-workmen quarried the stone on the Skibo estate, then skidded and hauled it over trails and roads to the railway. A Glasgow artisan fashioned the cross, and Mrs. Carnegie dictated the inscription—simple and unpretentious, it could not have been more appropriate:

ANDREW CARNEGIE
Born Dunfermline, Scotland
25 November, 1835
Died Lenox, Massachusetts
11 August, 1919

And that is all.

He composed his entire will himself. His wife and daughter had already been provided for. The servants in the New York home and the servants and workmen on the Skibo estate were all remembered, as were the heads of his various foundations. He had his way about our Presidents, after all. William H. Taft, the only ex-President living at the time of his death, recieved $10,000 a year for life; Mrs. Grover Cleveland and Mrs. Theodore Roosevelt each received $5000 yearly. Viscount Morley and David Lloyd George were given $10,000 annually. John Burns, a Labor Member of Parliament, who had attacked Carnegie bitterly at the time of the Homestead strike but who, as Carnegie thought, had served England well, received $5000 a year; and Thomas Burt, another Labor Member of Parliament, who had defended Carnegie against Burns's criticisms, was also given $5000.

Elihu Root, speaking at a memorial service held by the engineering societies of New York in the building which Carnegie had given them, said: "He belonged to that great race of nation-builders who have made the development of America the wonder of the world. . . . He was the kindliest man I ever knew. Wealth had brought to him no hardening of the heart, nor made him forget the dreams of his youth. Kindly, affectionate, charitable in his judgments, I wish that all the people who think of him as a rich man giving away money he did not need could know of the hundreds of kindly things he did, unknown to the world."

Index

Aberdeen University, 147
Acton, Lord, 139
Adams Express Co., 47, 48, 57, 66
Addison, Leila, 64
Addison, Mrs., 64
Aitken, Andrew, 1, 2, 10
Aitken, Mrs. Andrew, 1, 2, 8, 10, 13, 14
Allegheny, Pa., 15, 31, 51, 122
Allegheny Valley R.R., 27
Altoona, Pa., 43, 44, 51, 56, 58, 76
Anderson, Col. James, 31-34, 122, 153
Arnold, Mathew, 117, 136
Atlanta Library, 123

Balfour, Lord, 117
Bannockburn, Battle of, 5
Bar Harbor, 176
Bessemer Process, 93
Billings, J. S., 151
Bigelow, John, 176
Blaine, James G., 124, 128
Bottom Hooshiers, 16, 26, 82
Braddock, Pa., 96, 100, 113, 114, 132
Brooklyn Bridge, 105
Brooklyn Public Library, 151
Brooks, David, 19, 20-24, 27, 38, 39
Bryce, Lord, 117
Bull Run, Battle of, 70
Burns, John, 178
Burt, Thomas, 178

Campbell-Bannerman, Sir Henry, 117
Canmore, Malcolm, 5
Carnegie, Andrew, Birth, 3; disclaims coat of arms, 4; his heroes, 5; endows Lauder Technical College, 6;
George Lauder, Jr., 6; helps mother at shoe binding, 9; leaves Scotland for America, 12; works in textile mill, 16; Bottom Hooshiers, 16, 26, 82; works in bobbin factory, 17; studies double-entry bookkeeping, 19; offered job by telegraph company, 20; begins work as messenger, 23; suggests pooling boys' tips, 26; first raise in wages, 28; goes to Pittsburgh theatre, 31; writes to *Pittsburgh Dispatch*, 33; admitted to Anderson Library, 34; active in Sunday school, 35; Sunday skating, 36; takes first telegraph message, 38; sent to Greensburg as substitute, 40, 41; emergency duty in flood, 42; goes to work for Pennsylvania R.R., 43; Mr. Scott's "Andy", 44; dispatches trains after accident, 45; severity toward workmen, 46; father dies, 46; buys Adams Express stock, 47; joins Webster Literary Society, 50; moves to Altoona, Pa., 51, 52; meets Woodruff, sleeping-car inventor, 55-57; completes sleeping-car deal with Pennsylvania R.R., 57, 58; signs first promissory note, 58; made Superintendent of Western Division, 59-61; returns to Pittsburgh, 60, 61; moves to Homewood, 62; buys first oil property, 65, 66; official position in Civil War, 68; aids in retreat from Bull Run, 69-71; returns to railroad, 72; serious illness and vacation in Scotland, 72-

179

75; enters Keystone Bridge Co., 77, 78; organizes Cyclops Iron Works, 83; resigns from Pennsylvania R.R., 83; Union Iron Works organized, 83; organized Pittsburgh Locomotive Works, 84; buys more oil land, 84; walking tour of Europe, 85, 86; moves to New York City, 87-89; sells bridges, 89, 91; plans rest of life, 89, 90; makes deal with Pullman, 92, 93; begins benefactions, 97; panic of 1873, 97-100; stand against speculation, 99; buys summer home, 103; first meets Schwab, 103; Carnegie Brothers & Co. organized, 104; first Public Library, 105; coaching trip through Britain, 105, 106; takes over Homestead competitor, 108; invests with H. C. Frick, 110; first learns Schwab's name, 112; tells Schwab to raze converting mill, 115; becomes engaged to Miss Whitfield, 117; writes *Triumphant Democracy*, 118; buys newspapers in United Kingdom, 118; Miss Whitfield breaks engagement, 118; mother and brother die, 119; married, 119; gives Library to Edinburgh, 120; writes Gospel of Wealth, 121; gives Libraries to Allegheny and Pittsburgh, 122; gives Library to Atlanta, 123; gives organs to churches, 123, 158; builds Carnegie Hall, 123; gives Engineering Societies building, 123; delegate to Pan-American Congress, 124, 125; talks with President Harrison, 126-129; Homestead strike, 131-134; daughter Margaret born, 134; buys Skibo Castle, 135; life at Skibo, 136-138; pensions old railroad employees, 138; gives libraries in Scotland, 138; buys Lord Acton's library, 139, 140; breaks with Frick, 141, 142; sells Steel interests to J. P. Morgan, 144, 145; retires to devote life to philanthropy, 146, 147; gives New York libraries, 146, 151, 152; sets aside funds for Steel Works ex-employes, 146; Lord Rector of St. Andrews, 147, 165; sets up Scottish Universities Trust, 148; publishes *The Empire of Business*, 148; builds new home on Fifth Ave., 149; gives Brooklyn Library, 151; Carnegie Institute of Washington, 153; Hero Fund, 154-157; gives Taylor Hall to Lehigh University, 156-157; Church Peace Union, 158; Peace Palace at the Hague, 158; International Bureau of American Republics, 158; endows chairs and libraries at Universities, 159; buys Pittencrieff Glen, 159-161; Foundation for Advancement of Teaching, 162; Carnegie Corporation, 162, 170-173; Carnegie Foundation, 163; accepts Presidency of Peace Society, 166, 167; Carnegie Endowment for International Peace, 167; decorated by Foreign countries, 169; private pension list, 172, 173; endows British Fund, 173, 174; saddened by first World War, 175; gives libraries to American army camps, 176; daughter Margaret marries, 176; death, 177; will, 178.

Carnegie Institute (Pittsburgh), 122
Carnegie Institute (Washington), 153
Carnegie, Mrs. Louise Whitfield, 117-119, 134, 135, 143, 149, 171, 176, 177
Carnegie, Margaret, daughter, 134, 176
Carnegie, Margaret, mother, 8-11, 14, 15, 20, 21, 29, 30, 36, 40, 41, 48, 51-53, 60-63, 72, 73, 88, 89, 103, 106, 107, 109, 110, 119
Carnegie, Thomas, 12, 15, 29, 30, 60, 65, 66, 87, 88, 94-96, 119, 131
Carnegie, William, 3, 8, 9 13, 14-17, 20-22, 24, 30, 35, 36, 41-43, 46

Carnegie, Veterans Association, 149
Central Transportation Co., 87
Choate, Joseph, 176
Cleveland, Mrs. Grover, 178
Cluny Castle, 121, 135
Coal Washing Plant, 101
Coleman, Lucy, 87, 88
Coleman, William, 64-66, 84, 88, 95, 101
Cooper Institute, 138
Cornell University, 162
Columbia Oil Co., 66
Cowley, Alexander, 82
Cowley, William, 19, 34, 49, 82
Cresson, Pa., 103, 112, 118, 119
Cyclops Iron Works, 83

Denny, Dr. F. S., 119
Dunfermline, 3-7, 12, 14, 26, 72-74, 97, 102-106, 120, 136, 159-161, 173

Eads, Capt. James B., 84
Eastern Telegraph Co., 26, 41
Edinburgh Scotland, 5, 120
Edinburgh University, 147
Edward VII, King, 158
Elgin, Earl of, 117, 148
Exchange Bank of Pittsburgh, 98

Fort Sumter, 68
Franciscus, Mr., 45
Franciscus, Mrs., 51
Franks, John, 86
Franklin, Benjamin, 164, 165
Frick Coke Co., 131
Frick, Henry Clay, 109, 110, 131-142

Garrett, John W., 91
Gates, John W., 142
General Education Board, 163
Gilder, Richard Watson, 163, 176
Golden, John, 152
Gladstone, William E., 117, 118, 121, 136, 139, 140
Glasgow University, 148
Greensburg, town, 39, 41, 50, 67
Grey, Sir Edward, 136

Hague Peace Palace, 175
Harcourt, Sir William Vernon, 117
Harrison, Pres. Benjamin, 122-129
Hay, John (manufacturer), 17-22
Hay, John (statesman), 153, 158
Henderson, Mrs. John, 10, 11, 74
Hero Fund, 154-157
Hogan, Andrew, 14
Hogan, Mrs. Thomas, 8, 10, 13, 29
Hogan, Thomas, 10, 13, 14, 19-21
Homestead Mill, 108-114, 131-134, 178
Homewood, 62-64, 84, 87, 88, 95

Irvin, Agnes, 164, 165

Jones, Captain Bill, 100-113, 131, 149

Keystone Bridge Co., 77, 84, 89, 96
Kilgraston Castle, 120
Kloman, Andrew, 79, 81-83, 88, 94, 96

Lauder, George, Jr., 6, 75, 177
Lauder, George, Sr., 7, 9, 12, 13, 35, 72-75, 101, 102, 106, 119, 120, 160
Lauder Technical College, 6
Leonard, Jimmy, 39
Linville, H. J., 76, 84
Lombaert, General Superintendent, 43-46
Lucy Furnace, 94, 104

Macpherson, Cluny, 120, 121, 135
McCandless, David, 95, 96
McCargo, David, 26, 27, 44, 70
Mechanics' & Apprentices' Library, 32
Merchants' & Tradesmen's Institute, 138
Miller, Roswell, 176
Miller, Thomas N., 18, 19, 34, 47, 53, 54, 63-66, 72, 80-84, 88, 95, 138, 172
Missabe iron mines, 131
Moreland, William, 26, 27
Morgan, J. Pierpont, 142-145
Morgan, Junius S., 97

181

Morley, Viscount, 117, 140, 168, 175, 177
Morrison, Mary, 3, 146
Morrison, Thomas, 9-12, 102, 103
Morrison, William, 1, 2, 8, 10, 48

New York Central R.R., 56
New York Public Libraries, 146, 151-153

Oliver, Henry, 26, 27, 131

Paderewski, Ignace J., 136
Pan-American Congress, 124
Peacock, Alexander, 134
Pennsylvania R.R., 40-44, 50, 55, 68, 70-72, 76, 77, 83, 138
Phipps, Henry, 54, 80-82, 85, 88, 130, 133, 141, 142
Phipps, John, 18, 19, 34, 49, 54
Pitcairn, Robert, 26, 27, 44, 83
Piper, John L., 76, 88
Pittencrieff Glen, 159-161
Pittsburgh *Dispatch*, 33, 50
Pittsburgh Locomotive Works, 84
Pittsburgh, Pa., 2, 13, 22, 23, 26, 31, 38, 41, 48, 60-64, 72, 78, 94, 96, 122, 124
Prichett, Dr. Henry S., 173
Pullman, George M., 84, 91, 92

Radcliffe College, 164
Reid, James D., 26
Rockefeller, John D., 163
Rosebery, Prime Minister, 117, 120
Ross, Dr., 160, 161, 173
Roosevelt, Mrs. Theodore, 178
Root, Elihu, 169, 174, 176, 178

Saint Andrews University, 147
Saint Nicholas Hotel, 88, 89
School of Applied Design, 146
School of Applied Industries, 146
School of Applied Science, 146
Schiffler, Aaron, 77
Schwab, Charles, 103, 111-116, 132, 142-145, 150, 176

Scott, Thomas A., 43-48, 53, 68, 72, 77, 83, 87, 97, 98
Shadowbrook, 176
Shiras, George, 129
Singer, Mr., 108, 109
Skibo Castle, 135-138, 177
Sleepy Hollow Cemetery, 177
Southesk, Earl of, 4
Spencer, Herbert, 117
Stanton, Edwin M., 25, 159
Stewart, D. A., 62, 63, 95
Stewart, Rebecca, 53
Stokes, Mr., General Counsel, 67, 68
Strouse, David, 70
Sutherland, Duke of, 135-138

Taft, Mrs. William H., 178
Taylor, Charles, 155-157
Taylor Hall, 156, 157
Tchaikovsky, Peter, 123, 124
Tennant, Sir Charles, 136
Texas & Pacific R.R., 97-99
Thompson, J. Edgar, 44, 58, 76, 78, 83
Thompson, J. Edgar Steel Works, 97, 100, 104, 108
Tilden, Samuel J., 170
Triumphant Democracy, 118
Twain, Mark, 176

Union Iron Mills, 104
Union Pacific R.R., 84, 87, 92
United States Steel Co., 144, 145

Vandevort, John, 63, 66, 84

Watt, James, 148
Webster Literary Society, 50
Western Union Telegraph Co., 66
Whitfield, Louise (*see* Carnegie, Louise Whitfield)
Wilhelm II, Kaiser, 158, 175
Wilkins, Judge William, 63, 64
Wilson, James, 34, 49, 54
Woodruff Sleeping-car Co., 87
Woodruff, Theodore, 55-57, 66, 93
World War I, 175